With all good wishes –

Robin Reilly

12th November 1980 .

By The Same Author

Wedgwood Jasper

Wedgwood Portrait Medallions,
An Introduction

The Rest to Fortune,
The Biography of Major-General James Wolfe

The British at the Gates,
The New Orleans Campaign in the War of 1812

Wm. Pitt The Younger

with George Savage:

Wedgwood: The Portrait Medallions

The Dictionary of Wedgwood

Library of Congress Catalog Card Number: 80-82578

Printed in the United States of America

Design by Anthony Russell

Photography by Brent Burgess, Robert Golden, Gary Legget,
Ira Mandelbaum

No attempt has been made to give modern day equivalents in
sterling or dollars for any of the monetary figures cited in this
book. There is no accepted formula for taking into account
changes in valuation, inflation and other relevant conditions.

Acknowledgements

No work of this nature could be attempted without a great deal of assistance. The author and publishers acknowledge with gratitude the generous cooperation of Josiah Wedgwood & Sons Ltd., Josiah Wedgwood & Sons Inc., New York, and the Wedgwood Group of Companies, and in particular of Sir Arthur Bryan, Mr. Frederick de Costobadie, Mr. William Lydeard, Mr. William Taylor, Mr. Colin Wright, Mr. Raymond Smyth and Mr. Patrick Butterworth. Valuable practical help was also received at Barlaston from Mr. Derek Halfpenny, Miss Gaye Blake-Roberts, Mrs. Lynn Miller, Miss Sharon Ratcliffe, Mr. Brent Burgess and Mr. John Rainsford. Grateful thanks are also due to Mrs. Kathy Niblett (Assistant Keeper of Ceramics, City Museum & Art Gallery, Stoke-on-Trent), Miss Pamela Wood (Keeper of Applied Art, Nottingham Castle Museum), Mr. David Buten (Director, Buten Museum of Wedgwood), Mr. Eugene Buchanan and Mr. and Mrs. David Zeitlin for their assistance and for permission to photograph examples of Wedgwood ware in their collections or under their care.

The sources of Wedgwood ware photographed for this book are shown below.
Mr. Eugene D. Buchanan 190; Buten Museum of Wedgwood 6, 34, 51, 63, 76, 82, 90, 128, 135, 178, 223, 252, 254, 258, 283, 288-9, 297-8, 314-5, 317; Mrs. K. Niblett 100; Private collection 238; Nottingham Castle Museum 11, 46, 55, 154, 161, 180, 183, 194, 196, 198, 205, 207-13, 215, 217, 227, 231, 233, 235, 239, 244-5, 250-1, 279; Stoke-on-Trent Museum 12-15, 19, 22, 27, 32, 49, 53, 57-8, 64, 66, 92, 105-8, 113, 131, 144, 148, 152-3, 155, 157, 169, 177, 182, 191, 214, 216, 228, 240, 242, 253, 270, 273, 275-7, 316; Mr. and Mrs. D. Zeitlin 25, 47, 50, 78, 83, 99, 133, 164, 175, 246, 290; Author 26 (plates), 39-40, 43, 81, 93-4, 101-2, 111, 114, 116, 121, 124 (left), 129, 187, 249, 282, 306, 309; Wedgwood Museum, Barlaston all photographs not listed above.

1

2

3

4

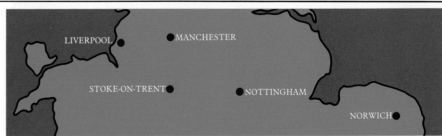

5

Casting. The process of forming shapes by pouring slip into d[...]
When sufficient thickness of the clay has adhered to the inside [...]
mold set to dry, after which the form is removed from the mold[...]

Cheese-Hard. The state (also known as 'leather-hard') of unfir[...]
content. In this condition, not unlike leather in firmness and pl[...]

Contents

Introduction

For more than 200 years the single word 'WEDGWOOD' has been the recognized trademark of the pottery founded by Josiah Wedgwood in 1759, and an internationally accepted guarantee of quality. The Wedgwood record of achievement is unique in industrial history. No other pottery or porcelain manufacturer has so powerfully influenced the industry of other countries, or made such a significant contribution to social change. With the production of Wedgwood's Queen's ware, tablewares of beauty and quality ceased to be the prerogative of the rich; and it is Wedgwood's Queen's ware, jasper, and black basalt that have been copied by manufacturers in Russia, Scandinavia, Germany, France and Italy.

The inscription on Josiah Wedgwood's memorial tablet in the Church of St. Peter's, Stoke-on-Trent, states that he 'converted a rude and inconsiderable manufactory into an elegant art and an important part of national commerce.' This discounts the beautiful early 18th century salt-glaze wares, and important work of a few master potters, among them Thomas Whieldon and Josiah's cousins, Thomas and John Wedgwood of the Big House, Burslem; but Josiah Wedgwood's responsibility for the transformation of the pottery industry is not in doubt.

The Collector's Wedgwood is designed to provide, for the first time, a visual history of Wedgwood wares from the founding of the firm to the present day. The enormous range of pieces produced during the past two centuries cannot ever be illustrated in full, but the collector who studies this book will be enabled to identify the style, type of body, and the period of all the most important wares. Knowledge of Wedgwood wares must be founded upon an understanding of quality, and primarily for this reason the illustrations include examples of great rarity which are unlikely to be seen outside museums; but an unusually high proportion of the photographs are of pieces which might be found in auction sales or antique shops by discriminating collectors with modest means.

Josiah Wedgwood was truly a man of his own time: shrewd, inventive, energetic, courageous and enterprising; a man without false modesty, confident in his strength but recognizing his limitations; a classic example of the vigor, creativity and resource that characterized the leaders of the Industrial Revolution in England. He founded a business that dominated the industry, and it has been alleged that the impetus he generated during his lifetime has sustained the Company's position in the forefront of that industry since his death. This is manifestly untrue. The briefest examination of the company's history reveals periods when neglect or the lack of more than ordinary vitality and imagination allowed other, better-managed, firms to take the lead, and more than one occasion when the factory was near to closure. It is one of the most remarkable aspects of the Wedgwood story that worthy successors have been found to build surely upon the foundations laid by Josiah I in the 18th century, continuing to create in their own time the traditions of the future.

RR
London, January 1980

I The Wedgwood Story

Josiah Wedgwood after the portrait by Sir Joshua Reynolds

To anyone familiar with old photographs or engravings of industrial England, 500 acres of woodland and pasture, bright in springtime with daffodils and flowering cherry trees, may seem an unlikely site for one of the world's most famous industries; but each day some 2,500 men and women make their way to such a country estate to work at the Wedgwood factory at Barlaston just three miles from the center of Stoke-on-Trent. Many come by car, others by bicycle or the local train to the 'Wedgwood Halt.' As late as the 1950s an intrepid member of the staff rode across the fields to tether his horse outside the main entrance, where the bronze statue of the first Josiah Wedgwood greets visitors to the factory.

The people of the Staffordshire Potteries, it is said, have clay in their veins. Warm-hearted and blunt-spoken, they offer friendship, loyalty and respect only to those who earn them. The Wedgwoods have been engaged in the pottery business for eleven generations, and there are men and women at Barlaston who can trace their family connections with the firm as far back as the 18th century. The first Josiah complained, in 1765, of being "teased with dilatory, drunken, idle worthless workmen," and he was later to impose fines for 'obseen and other writing upon the walls.' By his example, by factory discipline, and by his evident care for his employees and insistence upon fine quality in production and good working conditions, he created an atmosphere in which it was possible for workers to be part of a community and to feel proud of their work. Apart from one brief period early in the 19th century when Josiah's sons were away from the factory, his descendants and successors have sustained and strengthened this spirit, which has become an accepted part of the Wedgwood tradition.

Josiah Wedgwood was born in 1730, the youngest of the 13 children of Thomas and Mary Wedgwood of the Churchyard Pottery, Burslem.

The family had been craftsmen-potters for at least three generations, and the Church-yard Works had been built by Josiah's great-grandfather towards the end of the 17th century; but profits were small in the Staffordshire Potteries, ranging from about £90 to £300 a year, and few 'pot works' employed more than ten men. With some notable exceptions, these produced an uninspired assortment of simple black, brown or red jugs, mugs and butter-pots made from local clays, and a small quantity of salt-glazed stoneware.

Josiah began his education at the age of six, walking seven miles each day to school at Newcastle-under-Lyme; but three years later, on the death of his father, he went to work for his eldest brother, Thomas, who had inherited the Churchyard Pottery. At 14 he was officially apprenticed to learn 'the Art, Mistery, Occupation or Imployment of Throwing and Handleing.' He was handicapped by an infection in his right knee, resulting from an attack of smallpox which developed into osteomyelitis, and this later caused him to have the leg amputated under the supervision of his friend and 'favourite Aesculapius,' Dr. Erasmus Darwin. Unable to use the treadle which provided the power for the potter's wheel, Josiah turned his atten-tion to experiment. When, at the end of his apprenticeship, he was refused a partnership by his brother, he joined John Harrison and Thomas Alders for two unsatisfactory years at Cliff Bank. In 1754 he was taken into partnership by Thomas Whieldon of Fenton, at that time the most creative potter in Britain.

In the 24 years since Josiah's birth there had been important developments in the production and decorating of pottery. Whieldon made red wares, salt-glaze, and cream-colored ware, but his name is particularly associated with relief-molded wares and figures decorated with beautiful semi-transparent glazes, often applied to produce a mottled effect described as 'tortoiseshell.'

Wedgwood benefited from Whieldon's superior knowledge and experience, and it was during the period of their partnership that he began his own experiments, "to try for some more solid improvements as well in the Body as in the Glazes, the Colors, the Forms of the articles of our manufacture. . . I saw the field was spacious, and the soil so good, as to promise an ample recompense for any one who should labour diligently in its cultivation."

After five years with Whieldon, who generously allowed Josiah to retain, as his own property, the formulae of his experiments, Wedgwood started his own pottery at the Ivy House Works, rented for £10 a year. Three years later, in 1762, he moved to the Brick House, later known as the Bell Works because Wedgwood summoned his work-men by bell instead of the horn customary in the district.

During his time with Whieldon at Fenton Vivian, Wedgwood had perfected a green glaze for the decoration of the fashionable cabbage, cauliflower, melon and pineapple shapes first made in porcelain at Meissen in Germany and imitated at Chelsea in London. The formula, No. 7 in his Experiment Book, is dated 23 March 1759, less than five weeks before he established himself as an independent potter at the Ivy House, but it is clear that he continued to decorate ware at Whieldon's factory for some time after the official ending of the partnership. Green glaze wares had been produced in Staffordshire and Yorkshire previously, but Wedgwood's glaze was of brilliance and depth of color never achieved earlier.

In his first ten years in business on his own account Wedgwood also developed black basalt, a fine-grained stoneware infinitely superior to the coarse 'Egyptian black' of other Staffordshire potteries; improved and refined the 'variegated' wares made by Whieldon and others in imitation of such natural stones as agate and porphyry; and created an original cream-colored earthenware body which was to transform the pottery of Europe.

The name of Josiah Wedgwood is most closely identified with blue and white jasper, his most important ceramic invention, but incomparably his most lasting contribution to society, and to the industry of which he has been called the father, was his creamware which transformed the tablewares of Europe. It was, in his own words, 'a species of earthenware for the table, quite new in appearance, covered with a rich and brilliant glaze, bearing sudden alterations of heat and cold, manufactured with ease and expedition, and consqently cheap.'

He studied the shapes and design of contemporary silver and adapted them to the softer lines of earthenware, and he was not above emulating the best of Continental porcelain shapes, particularly from Sèvres in France. In a period when the English potters were directing their energy and invention towards the discovery of the secret of 'true' (hardpaste) porcelain, Josiah began to manufacture earthenware of excellence and distinction, creating a range of tableware that was at once cheap enough for families of quite humble means and yet elegant enough to be desired by royalty. In 1774, when Wedgwood issued his first tableware catalogue, his wholesale prices for plates were £1.00 for eight dozen, and for soup tureens seven shillings each. Wages for painters employed to decorate the ware varied between 14 shillings and £4.00 a week according to skill and seniority.

By 1765, the year in which Wedgwood was permitted by Queen Charlotte, consort of George III, to give his creamware the name 'Queen's ware' and to style himself 'Potter to Her Majesty,' he had already developed a market for his wares in America. As he wrote to Sir William Meredith, "The bulk of our particular manufacture is exported to foreign markets...and the principal parts of these markets are the Continent of Europe and North America...for the islands of North America we cannot make anything too rich and costly."

Page from Josiah Wedgwood's
Experiment Book

Early creamware vase and fruitwood
pattern. c. 1764

Block mold for a sauceboat

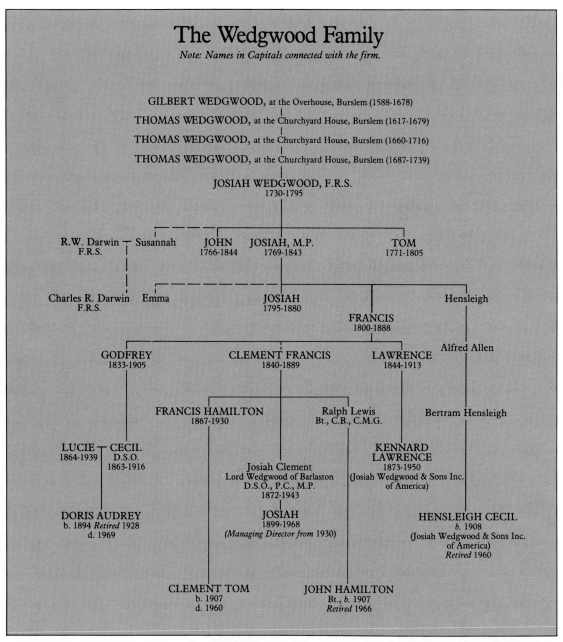

The Wedgwood Family

Note: Names in Capitals connected with the firm.

GILBERT WEDGWOOD, at the Overhouse, Burslem (1588-1678)

THOMAS WEDGWOOD, at the Churchyard House, Burslem (1617-1679)

THOMAS WEDGWOOD, at the Churchyard House, Burslem (1660-1716)

THOMAS WEDGWOOD, at the Churchyard House, Burslem (1687-1739)

JOSIAH WEDGWOOD, F.R.S.
1730-1795

R.W. Darwin — Susannah   JOHN   JOSIAH, M.P.   TOM
F.R.S.   1766-1844   1769-1843   1771-1805

Charles R. Darwin   Emma   JOSIAH   Hensleigh
F.R.S.   1795-1880

FRANCIS
1800-1888

GODFREY   CLEMENT FRANCIS   LAWRENCE   Alfred Allen
1833-1905   1840-1889   1844-1913

FRANCIS HAMILTON   Ralph Lewis   Bertram Hensleigh
1867-1930   Bt., C.B., C.M.G.

LUCIE — CECIL   KENNARD
1864-1939 | D.S.O.   LAWRENCE
        1863-1916   Josiah Clement   1873-1950
                  Lord Wedgwood of Barlaston   (Josiah Wedgwood & Sons Inc.
                  D.S.O., P.C., M.P.   of America)
                  1872-1943

DORIS AUDREY   JOSIAH   HENSLEIGH CECIL
b. 1894 *Retired 1928*   1899-1968   *b. 1908*
d. 1969   *(Managing Director from 1930)*   (Josiah Wedgwood & Sons Inc.
                                          of America)
                                          Retired 1960

CLEMENT TOM   JOHN HAMILTON
b. 1907   Bt., *b.* 1907
d. 1960   *Retired 1966*

Russia, too, became an important market. Largely due to the influence of Lord Cathcart, British ambassador to the Court of Catherine the Great, Wedgwood supplied a service of hand-painted *Husk* pattern to the Empress in 1770. Four years later he made for Catherine II the enormous 'Frog' service of 952 pieces, hand-painted in mulberry-colored enamel with 1,224 "real views of Great Britain." The service was intended for the palace of Chesman at La Grenouillère (the Frog Marsh) near Petrodvorets, and the border of each piece was painted with the emblem of a green frog (Plates 48-49). In 1779, in response to a demand for a whiter earthenware more closely resembling the appearance of porcelain, Wedgwood introduced 'Pearl' ware.

Wedgwood's black basalt bore little resemblance to the crude black ware already made by a number of Staffordshire potters. Smoother, and richer in hue, it was a handsome and much cheaper medium than bronze for classical vases, library busts, and bas-relief plaques and medallions, and it was also found attractive and suitable for such useful objects as kettles, coffeepots, and inkwells. Basalt proved to be remarkably versatile. It was a satisfactory ground for ornament and decoration in many styles and could be produced in a wide variety of objects from thinly-potted cups and cream jugs to massive baptismal fonts and vases more than four feet in height. Josiah's invention of a matte enamel for 'encaustic' painting, with which he decorated basalt vases in imitation of ancient red-figure vases, led to a brief but "violent *Vase madness*" among his most fashionable customers. In 1773 he wrote: "The Black is sterling and will last for ever," a bold forecast amply justified by the continuing popularity of basalt to the present day.

Two other colored stonewares or 'dry bodies' were introduced between 1765 and 1770: 'rosso antico,' a development from traditional red wares; and 'cane,' a beautiful golden-buff body scarcely recognizable as a descendant of Staffordshire brown earthenware. Both required further refinement before they reached the high standard demanded by Josiah, but both were to be important in the evolution of a distinctive range of ornamental pieces in neo-classical and Oriental styles.

In 1766 Wedgwood purchased for £3,000 the Ridge House estate between Newcastle-under-Lyme and Hanley. There he built a new factory, which he named Etruria. This was formally opened in June 1769. In the same year he took into partnership Thomas Bentley, a prosperous Liverpool merchant with whom he had formed a lasting friendship seven years earlier.

Born in the same year as Josiah, Bentley had been educated at the Presbyterian Academy at Findern, Derbyshire and, after apprenticeship to a Manchester firm of linen warehouse-men, had travelled on the Continent, acquiring fluency in French and Italian and a taste for antique art. In 1757 he had settled in Liverpool, where he had founded the firm of Bentley & Boardman, and as one of the Trustees he

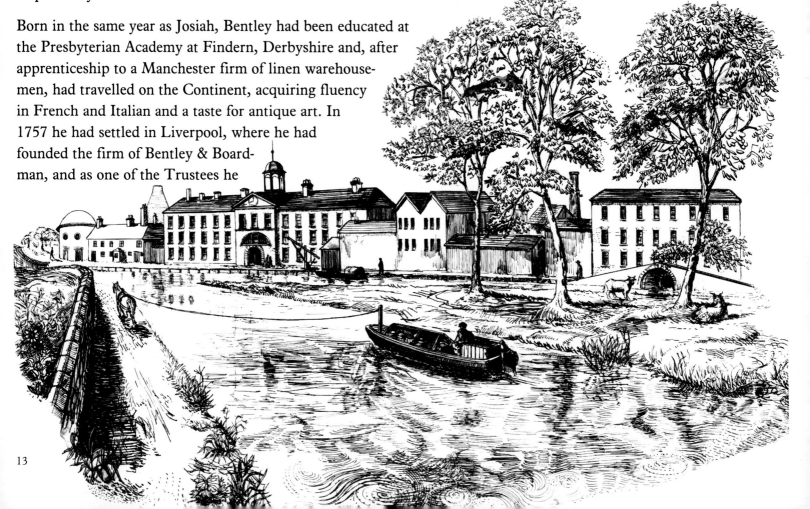

played a leading part in the founding of the Warrington Academy, for many years the center of intellectual activity in Lancashire and the home of liberal non-conformism. He was a frequent contributor to the *Gentleman's Magazine* and *Monthly Review,* and his charm, lively intelligence and wide interests brought him influential friends. By the middle of 1765 Bentley was providing Wedgwood with useful orders for export, and these steadily increased in volume until, in March 1767, Wedgwood was describing his friend as "a Pot mercht." Three months earlier Wedgwood had suggested a formal partnership and the deeds were signed on 10 August 1769.

The partnership concerned the manufacture of ornamental wares only since Josiah's cousin, Thomas Wedgwood, was already his partner in the production of 'useful' wares. This division was later the cause of a minor dispute which Wedgwood settled with his customary good sense, defining useful wares as generally those which would commonly be used at meals. Bentley was a man of education and taste, and his social contacts and knowledge of the arts were of inestimable value to Wedgwood. He took charge of Wedgwood's London showrooms and decorating studios, and was active in obtaining introductions to wealthy and influential patrons and in finding artists and modelers to work for Wedgwood at Etruria or, on commision, in London. The partnership lasted until Bentley's death, at the age of fifty, in 1780. As a partner and guide he was irreplaceable, and Wedgwood's letters to him, many of which have been preserved, are eloquent evidence of his influence and of the intimacy of their friendship.

Josiah had married, in 1764, his cousin, Sarah Wedgwood. Despite her precarious health, she bore him eight children, one of whom died in infancy, and outlived her husband, only four years her senior, by twenty years. A shrewd and considerate woman, she gave Josiah's life a necessary stability, and provided common sense and practical judgment on his designs of 'useful' wares for the table. In 1765, when he was perfecting his Queen's ware, Josiah wrote: "Sally is my chief helpmate in this as well as other things." Later he paid tribute to her influence: "I speak from experience in Female taste, without which I should have made but a poor figure among my pots, not one of which of any consequence is finished without the approbation of my Sally." Their sons, John and Josiah, were concerned with the Etruria factory after Josiah's death, and the youngest, Tom, is recognized as one of the inventors of photography. Their eldest daughter, Susannah ('Sukey'), married Dr. Robert Waring Darwin, son of Josiah's friend Erasmus, and became the mother of Charles Darwin, author of *Origin of the Species.*

It is plain from his correspondence that Josiah was a loyal and attentive husband and a devoted father. His letters to Bentley are filled with references to his wife's ailments and the progress of his children, of whom 'Sukey' was evidently his favorite. He had, however, little time to spare for them from his multitude of business activities. He seems to have been on the move frequently – to London, Liverpool, Cornwall or Derbyshire – jolting about uncomfortably in a coach over terrible roads, always in pursuit of trade or in search of new materials for his experiments. He was frequently in pain from

The Wedgwood family in the grounds of Etruria Hall, painted by George Stubbs

**Sarah Wedgwood, Josiah's wife,
by Sir Joshua Reynolds**

Typical of these were Wedgwood's early fruit and vegetable shapes decorated in green and yellow glazes, but the style is also apparent in the finials, spouts, handles and terminals of his early creamware pieces, and in his popular shell and shell-edge shapes. Josiah's personal interest in shells, which he collected, is evident in his use of shell motifs for relief decoration long after he had abandoned the rococo, of which the shell is almost the hallmark, for the neo-classical style.

Two of the leading exponents of the neo-classical style were the architects, James ('Athenian') Stuart and Robert Adam. Both had studied classical architecture and decoration at first hand; both published influential books illustrating their studies; both were friends of Josiah Wedgwood's; but it was Adam's interpretation of classical design that created the new style that Wedgwood was to follow. The Adam style was delicate, intimate, and elegant. Above all, he developed in interior decoration the use of pastel colors—soft blues and greens, lilac and yellow—as backgrounds for white plaster reliefs, generally of classical origin. This was Wedgwood's inspiration in his creation of jasper.

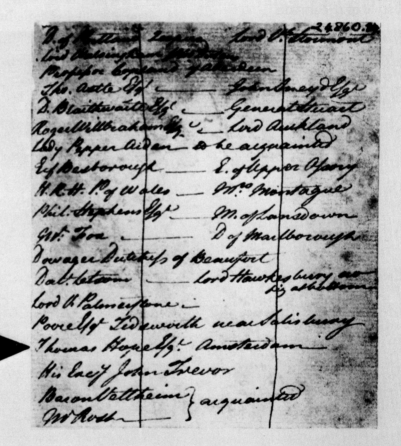

List of Subscribers to the Portland Vase, 1789

The enormous range of jasper produced during the past 200 years, and the smooth production line in the Barlaston factory today, using streamlined, but in all essentials the same manufacturing methods as those of the 18th century, give no hint of the complexity of Josiah's research. For more than four years, in which he made some 4,000 experiments, Wedgwood pursued his quarry with a driving energy, an intense passion, which drove him, in his own words, "almost crazy."

Two of his most intractable problems, those of differentiating between the sulphate and the carbonate of barium, and of eliminating impurities in his raw materials, would provide little difficulty under modern conditions; but he was experimenting with materials never recorded in use, materials of which little or nothing was known and for which there were but primitive methods of chemical analysis. He was further hampered by a patent to William Cookworthy of Plymouth in 1768, which granted him the sole use of Cornish stone and Cornish china clay. Josiah was obliged to look elsewhere for his raw materials, and his searches took him all over England.

As early as July 1767 he had despatched Thomas Griffiths to South Carolina to collect Cherokee clay, and this was subsequently used in Queen's ware, black basalt and jasper, though the quantity obtained was too small to allow for general production. In 1775 the patent, then owned by Cookworthy's successor, Richard Champion, was altered, largely at Wedgwood's instigation, to cover the use of Cornish clay in the manufacture of porcelain only, and Wedgwood no longer had to look further afield.

There can be little doubt that Wedgwood's original intention was to produce porcelain, and there is no doubt that he knew how to do so. His experiments, however, led him to an even more valuable discovery, and one which did not necessitate an infringement of the Cornish patent.

Wedgwood's mention to Bentley of experiments with a new white ceramic body in January 1771 was the first hint of an invention that was to absorb his thoughts and energy for nearly five years and take more than ten for its full development. After three years of intensive work he wrote to Bentley: "I have for some time been reviewing my experiments & I find such *Roots,* such *Seeds* as would open & branch out wonderfully if I could nail myself down to to the cultivation of them for a year or two. And the Fox-hunter does not enjoy more pleasure from the Chace..."; but four months later he was experiencing more trouble with his materials: "They have plagued me sadly of late. At one time the body is white & fine as it should be, the next we make perhaps, having used a different lump of the Spaith [barium] is a cinamon color. One time it is melted to a Glass, another time as dry as a Tob[acco] Pipe." Later he wrote, in some desperation, "If I had more *time,* and *hands,* & more *heads* I could do something — but as it is I must be content to do as well as I can. A man who is in the midst of a course of experiments *should not be at home* to anything, or anyone else but that cannot be my case. Farewell — I am almost crazy." Less than a month passed before he was able to report his ability to make "an excellent white body, & with absolute certainty." By September 1774 he had made the great breakthrough.

Blue and white jasper cameos of Hercules and Apollo mounted as buttons. c. 1785. Diameter 1¼ ins.

His difficulties were not over, but from then on they were generally confined to development and refinement. Although not yet completed, Josiah's great design — the invention of an original ceramic body — had been achieved.

No precise date can be given for the invention of jasper. It is first mentioned by name in a letter dated 27 November 1775, but it is clear that jasper was in limited production at least three months earlier. Ten months before he named it, he had written to Bentley that he was certain not only of the white body but also of blue, and "likewise a beautifull Sea Green, & several other colors *for grounds* to Cameos, Intaglios &c." In fact his troubles were not over: the jasper body continued to be fugitive and capricious, and a further problem was encountered when it was found that the colored grounds 'bled' into the white reliefs when they were fired. The introduction in 1778 of 'jasper dip' (a thin wash of colored jasper over a white ground or, more rarely, a ground of another color) helped to reduce the staining of reliefs and also served to increase the range and subtlety of coloring. A further refinement might be added by polishing. Wedgwood's jasper was as hard as natural stone (midway between turquoise and agate) and Josiah was therefore able to employ lapidary techniques to polish seals and cameos, and the interiors and rims of cups and bowls.

From 1776 until his death in 1795, much of Josiah's boundless energy was poured into establishing jasper in a bewildering variety of objects. Cameos and intaglio seals, already popular in basalt, were mounted in metal (many in cut-steel from the workshops of Matthew Boulton) for buckles, bracelets, brooches, coat-buttons, chatelaines, rings, sword hilts, and snuff boxes; medallions were set in boxes and desk sets of wood and papier mâché; larger medallions, plaques or tablets decorated coach panels, girandoles, furniture, grand pianos and chimney-pieces; and jasper in various shapes appeared as bell-pulls, door handles and finger-plates, and for the bases of ormolu and crystal candelabra. Un-mounted jasper pieces included candlesticks, flower pots, 'bough pots,' portrait medallions, plaques, tablets, tea and coffee wares ('Cab-inet pieces' not intended for use), figures, small busts, and, after 1780, a fine collec-tion of vases which, by 1795, numbered some 250 models.

The introduction of jasper vases was de-layed because relief ornament applied to curved surfaces tended to lift and buckle in firing. Josiah worked towards the solution of this problem by the appli-cation of simple ornament to smaller objects, such as bowls, cups and teapots. Sadly, Thomas Bentley, who had been instrumental in directing Wedgwood's choice of ornament towards the neo-classical, did not live to see the finest of all ceramic creations in this style.

Bentley's death deprived Josiah Wedgwood not only of his closest friend but also of his most trusted adviser in matters of taste. From 1780, al-though he pursued the development of his wares with undiminished energy, his invention flagged. Much of the

William Hackwood (c. 1757-1839), modeler at Etruria for 63 years

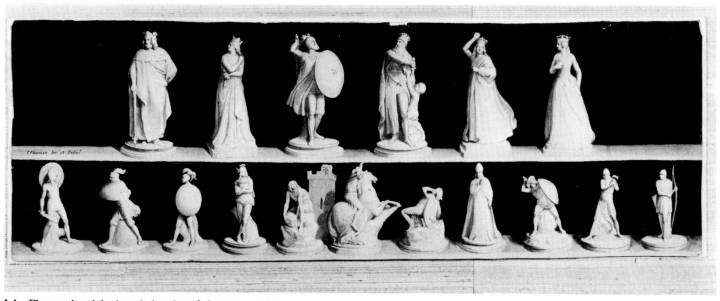

John Flaxman's original wash drawing of chessmen. 1785

most beautiful jasper, and all the jasper vases, were produced after the end of the partnership, but no new ceramic bodies were introduced, and progress appears to have been towards perfection of production rather than originality of design. It was a period of consolidation, when Josiah built upon the foundations laid between 1759 and 1780, securing his reputation and the future of his successors. His children were growing up: his eldest son, John, worked in the factory as early as 1781, and the younger Josiah reported to his father on trials of cane ware when he was only 14. Later, soon after he came of age, he was to travel on the Continent, to show the Wedgwood Portland vase at the Courts of Europe.

Of all the vases produced by Wedgwood, the one which has become most famous and which brought him the greatest public acclaim was his copy of the Portland vase. Of the early history of the original vase little is known. A superb example of cameo-cut cased glass, it is believed to have been made c.27 BC - 14 AD, probably by Alexandrians in Italy. The meaning of the relief figures is uncertain, though it is now thought that they represent the marriage of Peleus and Thetis, and the medallion on the base is not of the same date as the body, which was originally of amphora shape.

The vase is first recorded in the possession of the Barberini family in 1642, and it was acquired from them by James Byres, a Scottish antiquary and entrepreneur, in 1780. He sold it for £1,000 to Sir William Hamilton, connoisseur and complaisant husband of Nelson's mistress, whose collection of ancient red-figure vases, sold to the British Museum in 1772, had already provided inspiration for Wedgwood's 'encaustic' painted basalt vases. Hamilton, in need of money, disposed of the vase to the eccentric Duchess of Portland, whom Horace Walpole described as 'a simple woman, but perfectly sober, and intoxicated only by *empty* vases.' Following her death, Wedgwood was granted permission by her son to borrow the vase for twelve months for the purpose of making replicas in jasper.

For four years Josiah worked on the task himself, aided by his son, Josiah II, and his senior resident modelers, William Hackwood, Henry Webber and William Wood, and for it he created a special blue-black jasper to match as nearly as possible the shade of the original. The first copies, one of which was inspected and officially approved by Sir Joshua Reynolds, President of the Royal Academy, were produced in 1790. Of the first edition, the precise number of which is unknown (though 26 orders were accepted), 16 are known to have survived.

Blue and white jasper button, ornamented with one of the models of horses by Edward Burch after drawings by George Stubbs. c. 1790

There can be no doubt that the replicas of the Portland vase made by the first Josiah Wedgwood represent a *tour de force* of the potter's craft. Aesthetically their value is questionable. The proportions of the original are marred by its truncation from an amphora to its present squat shape, presumably the result of restoration after breakage some time before 1642, and its beauty lies largely in the exquisite quality of the cameo-cutting, through a layer of white glass to the blue-black ground. Wedgwood's figures, though superbly modeled and finished, were applied, and it is impossible to reproduce in a ceramic body the distinctive purity and luminosity of glass. Most of the later editions are generally not remarkable for delicacy of modeling, and have little appeal for the true collector. For the edition of 1839, in deference to a public taste zealously guarded against the spectacle of frontal nudity of whatever classical respectability, the figures were draped, a sober reminder of the idiocies perpetrated in the name of morality.

Two editions deserve special mention: that of 15 fine copies taken from the original molds and finished by the glass engraver, John Northwood, in 1877-80; and the much larger edition completed by Harry Barnard between 1923 and 1930. A small number of solid green and white jasper vases was made in 1957, and a limited edition of 50 in the new Portland blue was issued in 1973. Since 1878 the Portland vase outline has been used in printed form as the company's backstamp for bone china. The original Portland vase was deliberately smashed in February 1845 by an Irishman who claimed that he

Etruria in Staffordshire Jan'y 26 1787

His Grace the Duke of Bedford

Bought of Josiah Wedgwood,

Potter to her Majesty

Black and white jasper plaque by George Stubbs, *The Fall of Phaeton*, c.1785

was suffering from a hangover. It has twice been restored, and is now displayed in the British Museum in London.

Wedgwood's production of the Portland vase is generally regarded as the crowning achievement of his life, the triumphant outcome of twenty years of experiment and development in the use of jasper. During this period he had perfected the ceramic body, introduced an attractive range of colors, and exploited with admirable effect various methods of decorating and ornamenting, many of which had been originally used with basalt. It was, however, in the ornaments themselves, and in his employment of artists, that Josiah showed his awareness of the importance of his invention, creating a form of decoration that has long outlived the fashion that was its inspiration.

Before the invention of jasper, Wedgwood bought copies of antique bas-reliefs from the London makers of plaster casts. For his first medallion portraits of contemporaries, he sought out the modelers of wax portraits, reproducing basalt medallions from plaster casts and occasionally commissioning original work, including portraits of himself and Thomas Bentley from Joachim Smith, a well known modeler in wax. All such models required adaptation and finishing at Etruria, and for this Wedgwood relied principally upon William Hackwood. The introduction of jasper made it necessary to commission work not generally available to other manufacturers.

Hired as an 'ingenious boy' in 1769, and doubtfully permitted to model his first portrait two years later, Hackwood rapidly made himself indispensible. By July of 1776 Wedgwood was already wishing he had "half a dozen more Hackwoods." Apart from finishing a very large number of busts and remodelling or adapting quantities of designs by other artists, Hackwood created important original work. He retired in 1832, completing an astonishing 63 years of service to the firm.

The most famous of Wedgwood artists in the 18th century was John Flaxman. The son of a modeler and maker of plaster casts from whom Wedgwood obtained models and casts, the younger Flaxman suffered in childhood from ill-health. He won the first prize of the Royal Society of Arts in 1767, when he was only twelve years old, and exhibited at the Royal Academy three years later. He was elected a member in 1800 and became Professor of Sculpture in 1810. By 1775 he was working for Wedgwood, who wrote to Bentley in January: "I am glad Flaxman is so valuable an Artist. It is but a few years since he was a most supreme Coxcomb." A year later Josiah was advising his partner to "give Flaxman a head or two to Model as it may excite our Modelers emulation." It was Flaxman who advised Wedgwood about the plaster decorations for the rooms of Etruria Hall, and in 1787 Wedgwood subsidized his extended stay in Rome, where he supervised the work of modelers employed there to copy antique bas-reliefs for reproduction in jasper. Flaxman never worked at Etruria, which he appears to have visited only once during his association with Wedgwood.

Wedgwood's production in the 18th century would have looked very different without the work of Flaxman. He modeled a large number of the most important portrait medallions, and

bas-reliefs for cameos, medallions and tablets as well as figures, chessmen and vases; his contribution to the artistic development of jasper was supreme. His relationship with Wedgwood provides an interesting illustration of the friendly association between artist and manufacturer.

Flaxman accepted Wedgwood's suggestions and criticisms, adapting his technique to reproductive processes and benefiting from the disciplines imposed by them. A superb draughtsman, modeler and sculptor, Flaxman was, until recently, more celebrated on the continent of Europe than in his own country.

Another artist whose fame today far exceeds his success in his lifetime is George Stubbs. His work for Wedgwood does not compare in importance with Flaxman's, and he exercised no lasting influence on Wedgwood design, but his two fine bas-reliefs for basalt and jasper, and his enamel paintings on large unglazed Queen's ware plaques, are among the rarest and most highly prized of all Wedgwood objects. Of particular interest to the Wedgwood historian are the portraits on Queen's ware plaques of Josiah and his wife, Sarah, and the painting in oils on panel of Josiah with his family in the grounds of Etruria Hall (Pages 14-15).

Josiah II, second son of Josiah I, and partner at Etruria from 1790 to 1843
After the portrait by William Owen R.A.

Wedgwood's production of Queen's ware plaques, the largest of which was 30 inches x 41½ inches, was a considerable technical achievement. The first was sent to Stubbs in London in December 1777, and from 1780, when Stubbs visited the factory, until Josiah's death in 1795, plaques were supplied regularly. Stubbs modeled two bas-reliefs, *The Frightened Horse* (1780) and *The Fall of Phaeton* (c.1785); 19 small relief studies of horses were modeled by Edward Burch, probably from the original drawings by the artist.

Henry Webber, a distinguished sculptor, was head of the ornamental department at Etruria from 1784 to 1806. To him are attributed some of Wedgwood's finest figures, including those of Diana and Minerva and the magnificent Britannia group (Plate 238). The models of Flaxman, Hackwood and Webber were classical in style. The romantic or 'sentimental' taste of the late 18th century was principally satisfied by the designs of three amateur artists: Lady Diana Beauclerk (daughter of the second Duke of Marl-borough), Lady Templetown, and Miss Emma Crewe.

In 1790, the year in which the first copies of the Portland vase were completed, Josiah took his three sons into partnership and prepared to retire from the business. He died on 3 January 1795. His life had been full. His liberal attitudes had led him to support the American Revolution, the campaign for the abolition of the slave trade, and, in its early stages, the French Revolution. In March 1778 he lamented "the absurdity, folly and wickedness of our whole proceedings with America," and later in the year wrote to Bentley that he "bless'd my stars and Lord North that America was free," and added, "I rejoice most sincerely that it is so."

The Society for the Suppression of the Slave Trade was founded in 1787, and Wedg-wood became a member of the committee. Thomas Clarkson, one of the leaders of the movement for abolition, paid tribute to Wedgwood's active support: "He made his own manufactory contribute to this end...He took the seal of the committee...for his model, and he produced a beautiful cameo." Modeled by Hackwood, the cameo depicted a manacled black slave, kneeling, with his hands raised in supplication, and bore the inscription 'Am I not a man and a brother?' Clarkson wrote: "Some had them inlaid in gold in the lid of their snuff-boxes. Of the ladies, several wore them in bracelets, and others had them fitted up in an ornamental manner as pins for their hair. At length the taste for wearing them became general, and thus fashion...was seen for once in the honorable office of promoting the cause of justice, humanity, and freedom."

Josiah's interest in the Duke of Bridgewater's Trent and Mersey canal, of which he was one of the foremost promoters, was less altruistic. Roads in the area were little better than cart tracks, often impassable in winter, and before the construction of the canal the pack horse was widely used for the transport of both raw materials and finished products. The canal, completed in 1777 after eleven years of constructional work, was 93 miles long, linking the Potteries with Liverpool and Hull. It passed through the Etruria estate, with a branch alongside the factory, and reduced the cost of transportation from tenpence to 1¾ pence per mile per ton for Wedgwood's raw materials.

In January 1783 Josiah was elected Fellow of the Royal Society. Eight months earlier he had read to the Society the first of five papers, two relating to the chemistry of clays and three describing his invention of a new instrument for measuring high temperatures. This pyrometer, originally invented to enable kiln masters to judge the temperature of potters' kilns, was the first instrument to provide anything like an accurate estimate of temperatures beyond the range of the mercury thermometer and had, therefore, a much wider application in other scientific fields than in the pottery industry.

Print from Ackermann's *Repository of the Arts* showing the showrooms of Wedgwood & Byerley at York Street, London, 1810

Without the advantages of social rank at birth or much formal education, Wedgwood had gained the respect and friendship of aristocratic patrons, including Sir William Hamilton, whose influence was certainly important in Josiah's conversion to neo-classicism, and others whose collections of antiquities were made available to him for copying. By his methods of production and factory organization, Wedgwood brought the Industrial Revolution to the Potteries. He was, more than any man, responsible for converting the craft of pottery into an industry. By painstaking inquiry, and experiment, he transformed existing ceramic bodies and glazes, and created jasper, an original body which has a far wider and more enduring appeal than the fashion that gave rise to it. By employing. or commissioning, some of the best artists and modelers in the country, Josiah forged a lasting link between artist and craftsman. In a speech in 1863, William Ewart Gladstone, the Liberal statesman who was, himself, a collector of Wedgwood ware, said of Josiah Wedgwood: 'he was the greatest man who ever, in any age or country, applied himself to the important work of uniting art with industry.' It was a fitting epitaph.

Queen's ware 'Glacier,' c. 1803

After Josiah's death the Etruria factory was left for some years to the management of Tom Byerley, his nephew. John Wedgwood had withdrawn from the partnership in 1793, and neither he nor his younger brother, Josiah II, showed any desire to give up their lives as country gentlemen to return to the Potteries. Tom, the youngest and most brilliant of Josiah's sons, had also withdrawn in 1793, and he died in 1804. The French Revolution, the Napoleonic Wars, and deteriorating relations with the United States, culminating in the War of 1812, had seriously damaged trade throughout Europe, and Josiah II thought the business not worth continuing. Byerley was no substitute for the first Josiah. The result of trade recession and poor management was a frightening decline in factory discipline and manufacturing standards.

John rejoined the firm as a partner in 1800, but it was not until 1804 that he returned to live in Staffordshire. His letters to his brother, Josiah II, reveal a sorry state of affairs at Etruria. "There are," he wrote in February, "many things that may be done...When I was at the works this last week I found the clay was in miserable order...The whole system of the ovens also requires a fresh arrangement." Next month he was reporting 60 dozen plates spoiled from one oven and 40 dozen from another, "and the men seemed to consider that as a very fair sample of firing."

John set about the task of restoring discipline and standards of production. He was joined by Josiah II in 1806, and it is clear that their joint efforts saved the firm from final failure. The production of Queen's ware, jasper, basalt, cane and rosso antico were continued, but new types of ware were introduced: a colored 'dry body' called 'Drab ware'; the first Queen's ware colored body (Celadon), and underglaze blue printed patterns on Pearl ware in 1805; lustre in 1806; bone china in 1812, (withdrawn about 1828); and smear-glaze on cane, drab, and white stone wares, all of which might be ornamented in contrasting colors of blue, green, lilac or chocolate. Some of these were innovations of lasting importance, and they give some indication that the spirit of the first Josiah was not entirely lacking in his sons.

In addition, basalt and rosso antico were given an altered appearance with new 'Egyptian' hieroglyphic reliefs and, from 1810, enameled decoration in the Chinese *famille rose* style. Pastry ware was introduced at the time of acute flour shortage, and the cane ware game-pie dishes became extremely popular. Of this period (c.1800) a contemporary biographer of Beau Brummel wrote: 'The scarcity. . . was so great that the consumption of flour for pastry was forbidden in the Royal Household. . . and Wedgwood made dishes to represent piecrust.' Later in the 19th century, equipped with 'liners' (separate vessels shaped to fit inside the dishes), they became forerunners of Wedgwood's oven-to-table ware.

By their efforts Josiah II and John saved the business, but they were unable entirely to reverse the decline resulting from unfavorable trade conditions and increasing competition. Their bone china failed. They had produced it reluctantly in response to public demand at a time when their competitors were marketing china at prices little above Wedgwood's best Queen's ware. The demand was for "a dazzling mixture of color with gold in broad shades covering the whole ware," according to Thomas

Queen's ware plaque painted by Thomas Allen. Signed and dated 1891

Byerley's son who had become manager of the London showrooms. The Wedgwoods found themselves unable to break away from the restraints of their neo-classical heritage to conform to the opulent taste of the Regency. Their bone china patterns were beautiful, but they were not fashionable. In 1828, as an expedient of doubtful economy, the London showrooms were closed, and worse, the irreplaceable stock of models and molds stored there was sold. John had retired again in 1812, but he lived in Staffordshire until 1825. None of his four sons were associated with the business.

In 1823 Josiah II's son, Josiah III, was taken into partnership, and he was succeeded by his younger brother Francis, whose branch of the family provided the senior partners in the firm until 1895, when the company was incorporated. This was a period of useful technical advancement. Carrara, Wedgwood's name for unglazed 'statuary' porcelain marketed by other manufacturers under the name of 'Parian', was introduced in 1848 for figures, groups and busts; the Lavender colored body was perfected for tableware in 1850; and majolica, a form of 'art pottery' decorated with colored glazes, made its first appearance ten years later. Most notably, the Wedgwoods rose to the challenge of increasing competition and reintroduced bone china in 1878. It has been, ever since, an essential part of Wedgwood's production, particularly for the North American market.

It is significant, as a measure of the firm's revival, that two of the finest ceramic artists in the country, Thomas Allen and Emile Lessore, joined Wedgwood from the Minton factory. Allen, who worked at Etruria from 1876 to 1905, as Art Director from 1880, was widely regarded as the leading Staffordshire figure painter of the 19th century. His principle work – decorous and chastely draped semi-nudes popular among Victorian art-lovers who, nevertheless, covered the legs of pianos in case they should appear erotically stimulating – appears on large vases, two of which were shown at the Paris Exposition of 1876, where Wedgwood gained a gold medal. Lessore, who had worked at the Sèvres factory, was engaged by Francis Wedgwood in 1858. From 1863 to 1875 he worked as a freelance for Wedgwood and on his own account, but from 1868 he lived in France because he could not stand the English climate. He painted Queen's ware and majolica in a highly individual style, free and spontaneous, owing something to the Barbizon school. His work, now highly prized, was appreciated in his own lifetime and was bought by Victorian collectors as an investment.

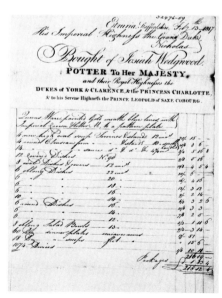

Invoice for ware supplied to the
Grand Duke Nicholas of Russia, 1817

In 1880 Wedgwood began to make for Jones, McDuffee & Stratton Co. of Boston the first of more than 1,000 commemorative historical views printed on Queen's ware plates and dishes specifically for sale in the United States of America. These were advertised as 'excellent for the plate rail effect,' but it would be a mistake to dismiss them as mere souvenirs. The quality of engraving was excellent, and the many sets comprise a remarkable series of 'named views' which will not be without historical value. In this period, too, Wedgwood introduced bronze and gold ornaments for black basalt, and a bronze basalt body ornamented with traditional reliefs in gold. Both were influenced by the contemporary fashion for Japanese bronzes.

Important marks, printed or impressed in the body, which are of considerable assistance in dating Wedgwood ware, made their first appearance in the 19th century. The most noteworthy of these are the Registry mark (1842-83), the three-letter date mark on earthenware (1860-1929), and the addition to the WEDGWOOD trademark of the words

'ENGLAND' and 'MADE IN ENGLAND' (1891 and 1898). These are shown in detail and explained with other marks in Chapter 4.

The turn of the century found the company once more in difficulties. The Spanish-American War had depressed business in North America, and two directors, Cecil and Frank Wedgwood, were away in South Africa, serving in the Boer War. In 1906 Kennard Wedgwood went to live in the United States, and 13 years later he founded the subsidiary Wedgwood company in New York. On their return from the war, Cecil and Frank set about the task of reviving the company's fortunes. In this they were greatly assisted by employment of John Goodwin as Art Director, and a prestigious order for a state dinner service for the White House. Alfred and Louise Powell, the latter a granddaughter of Emile Lessore, created new styles in Wedgwood design and founded a school of free-hand painting at Etruria. Their work, which owed much of its inspiration to William Morris and the designers of the Arts and Crafts movement, was in the English pottery tradition but marked a clear departure from Wedgwood's modern factory production.

Another, and commercially even more important, departure was achieved with the introduction of the lustre patterns designed by Daisy Makeig-Jones. In 1912 a real technical breakthrough had been made when powder blue (a sponged color, producing a stippled effect in imitation of the Chinese) was perfected for bone china. Daisy Makeig-Jones, an eccentric artist and designer at Etruria whose early work had shown no hint of particular talent or invention, was inspired to use the powder colors as backgrounds to designs enriched by the use of lustre. Her first 'Ordinary Lustres' were fairly conventional designs of dragons, birds, fish, fruit, or butterflies, but in 1916 she produced the first of her now famous 'Fairyland Lustre' patterns. For the next 13 years these designs poured from the studio, and with them Wedgwood assumed, for the first time, the lead in the production of ornamental bone china. By the end of 1920, the company's deficit, £25,000 in 1903, had been converted to a surplus of £14,000, a transformation achieved in spite of the First World War, in which Cecil had been killed.

Statue of Josiah Wedgwood by Edward Davies, which stands at the entrance to the Barlaston factory

Between 1927 and 1931 four young members of the family—Josiah V (son of Lord Wedgwood of Barlaston), Tom (Frank's son), John (now Sir John Wedgwood Bt.) and

Hensleigh (President of the New York Company 1947-60) – joined the Company. Josiah was only 31 when he succeeded Frank as Managing Director. The arrival of the new generation of directors coincided with the worst slump in the history of the pottery industry, following the Wall Street crash of 1929. During the next decade, while many other firms closed their factories, Wedgwood was saved by the courage and resolute action of the young directors and the inventiveness of Norman Wilson, who had joined the Company as Works Manager in 1927. Stringent economies were made, new designers commissioned, and methods of production modernized. The designs of resident Art Director, Victor Skellern, and of such distinguished outside designers as John Skeaping, Keith Murray, Arnold Machin and Eric Ravilious, created for Wedgwood a public image that was at once relevant to contemporary taste and, in quality of design and production, in accord with the Company's history and reputation. This was a period of genuine creativity, unrivaled since the time of the first Josiah and accurately following his policy, when Wedgwood gave meaning to the 'living tradition' that became the declared policy of the Company.

Hon. Josiah Wedgwood (Josiah V), Managing Director 1930-64 and Chairman 1947-67

By 1935 the progressive subsidence of the Etruria factory was causing grave concern. The evident success of their policies persuaded the directors to take the crucial decision to follow the founder's example and build a new factory. An estate of 382 acres (later extended to 500 acres) near Barlaston village was purchased in 1937, and the foundation stone was laid on 10 September 1938. Building was interrupted by the Second World War, in which John and Hensleigh Wedgwood and Norman Wilson served, but the factory, the first in Britain to use electric tunnel ovens for firing the ware, was completed in 1949.

Modernized methods of production and new trends in design required the creation of fresh shapes and patterns. Lithography was introduced for the decoration of Queen's ware and bone china, and Victor Skellern's designs were augmented by those of Peter Wall and Robert Minkin (now Art Director), and of outside artists, notably Richard Guyatt, Edward Bawden and Lawrence Whistler. Wedgwood's London showrooms, re-opened in 1875, had been given up during the war, but new premises in Wigmore Street were acquired in 1947, and the first of the Wedgwood Rooms, specialist Wedgwood shops in department stores, was opened in 1953.

More than ever before the American influence on Wedgwood design and marketing became apparent, particularly in the 'Bridal' market for bone china, and this influence quickly extended into the field of collecting. With few exceptions, the finest pieces from great British collections of Wedgwood dispersed in the 25 years after the war were acquired for collections in North America.

Among those who joined Wedgwood's sales force at the end of the war was Arthur

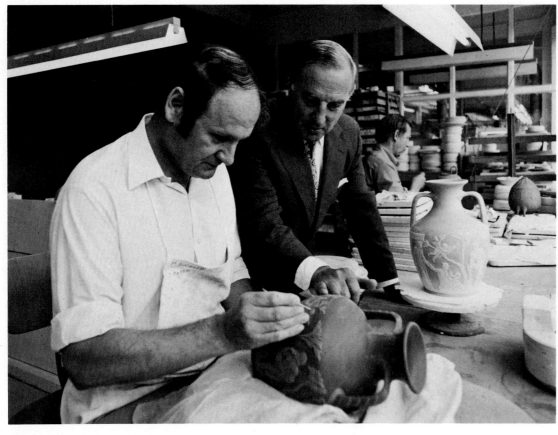

Bryan, demobilized from service in air crew with the Royal Air Force. In 1960, after
seven years as London Manager, five as General Manager of the Wedgwood Rooms,
and a year as General Sales Manager for all markets, he succeeded Hensleigh
Wedgwood as President in New York. Three years later he returned to England as
Managing Director of the parent Company. In 1968, he succeeded Josiah V as Chairman. Earlier in the year the Company's shares were introduced for the first time to the
London Stock Exchange.

Since 1966 the Company has been engaged in almost continuous planned expansion.
The Wedgwood Group of companies was formed with the acquisition of the businesses
of William Adams, Royal Tuscan and Susie Cooper. Further acquisitions, which have
included two glass factories, have more than doubled the Group's size in 14 years, and
in 1979 Wedgwood expanded in America by purchasing the assets of the Franciscan
manufactory in Glendale, California. Plans had already been made to complete, by the
end of 1980, a $20 million development program to increase production capacity in
England by more than 25 per cent and the number of employees to more than 10,000.

Throughout this period of expansion under the Chairmanship of Sir Arthur Bryan
(knighted in 1976 for services to export), Wedgwood has maintained and strengthened
its international reputation for quality and inventiveness, reaffirming the belief of the
directors that a living tradition is one which is continuously reborn.

2

Wedgwood Wares
I. Earthenware

Queen's Ware

Josiah Wedgwood's creamware, known since 1765 as Queen's ware, was intended primarily for the production of 'earthenware for the table.' He described it in 1763 as "quite new in appearance," although some fine creamware had been made elsewhere in England for some years. His earliest creamware was of a rich buff color, and the glaze, which had a distinctive greenish tinge, suffered from crazing. By 1763 he had produced a creamware of a paler shade, but it was during the following five years that he perfected his Queen's ware by the addition of Cornish china clay and china stone into the body and glaze. Queen's ware of this period, and for the next 25 years until Josiah's death, was pale cream in color and light in weight, and the brilliant glaze, still tinged with green, was applied thinly and evenly to eliminate crazing.

Green Glaze and Cauliflower. To Josiah's first ten years in business on his own account also belong most of the green and yellow glazed wares in fruit and vegetable forms (Plates 11, 12, 14). The green glaze was used for a variety of molded leaf shapes in addition to the apple, pear, melon, pineapple and cauliflower pieces. Many of these forms were made by other potters, but Wedgwood's were more finely detailed and the glaze has a more lustrous appearance. When Queen Charlotte ordered a creamware tea and coffee service for twelve in 1765, she stipulated that it should include matching melons (covered preserve dishes with leaf stands).

Variegated. While he was refining his Queen's ware. Josiah was beginning to make decorative vases. A few extremely rare early examples have survived, decorated with engine-turned patterns and bearing traces of gilding (Plate 2). Less scarce, but highly valued by collectors, are those described as 'variegated' or 'crystalline.' Variegated wares were made by one of three techniques: by wedging colored clays together to form a marbled or striated body; by mixing colored clay slip on the surface of the ware; or by mingling colors in the glaze, usually by dusting the body with metallic oxides before glazing. The first method produced 'marbled' or 'solid agate' ware (Plates 19, 20); the second and third yielded the surface decorations in imitation of natural hardstones and known, according to coloring, by such names as 'porphyry,' 'granite,' 'pebble,' and 'surface agate.' The production of these vases continued throughout the period of the Wedgwood & Bentley partnership, and many were mounted on basalt or white jasper plinths. Decorative handles and applied ornament were of creamware, and these often show traces of gilding. Vases of this type were also made in the 19th century, but their quality was poor in comparison with those made during the lifetime of Josiah I. Some interesting marbled pieces were part of the Norman Wilson Unique ware made between 1932 and 1963 (Plate 26).

Transfer-printed. As early as September 1761, Wedgwood began to employ Sadler & Green of Liverpool to decorate his creamware with transfer-prints. An invoice from Sadler dated April 1764 charges £64 for the decoration of 1,760 pieces, and it is clear from the accounts that Sadler & Green bought plain Queen's ware from Wedgwood to decorate and sell from their Liverpool warehouse. By 1771 invoices for printing were averaging about £650 a month, and the value of plain Queen's ware supplied amounted to almost as much. When John Sadler retired in 1770, Wedgwood was doing some printing in his Chelsea Decorating Studios, and within ten years he was employing his own engravers, but Guy Green continued to print for Wedgwood until 1793. The subjects of these prints were extremely varied and included Masonic insignia, portraits of royalty or popular heroes (e.g. George III, Queen Charlotte, Frederick the Great, General Wolfe, John Wesley), and reproductions of such well-known engravings as *The Tithe Pig, The Tea Party,* and the *Death of Wolfe* (from Woollett's engraving after the painting by Benjamin West). (Plates 31-33).

Underglaze blue printing was not attempted until 1905, when a few fine botanical prints, including the exceptional *Water Lily* design (Plates 112, 115), and patterns inspired by the popularity of Chinese decoration were made. These were produced on Pearl ware to avoid discoloration of the blue print. Transfer-printing has been continued until the present day with such popular patterns as *Willlow* (1818), *Landscape* (1832) and *Ferrara* (1832), all still in production on Queen's ware, and commemorative wares. (Plate 40). Many of Wedgwood's tableware patterns are transfer-printed in outline before enameling, but since 1944 the use of lithography has been more frequent.

Enameled. As the Sadler & Green invoices show, Wedgwood's monochrome transfer-printed ware was a popular success, but he needed color to appeal to feminine taste and to compete with the more highly decorative porcelain services of Meissen, Sèvres and Chelsea. During the 1760s he supplied the firm of Robinson & Rhodes in Leeds with Queen's ware for enameling. In 1768 David Rhodes became Josiah's tenant in premises in Newport Street, London, and for the next nine years he appears to have worked exclusively for Wedgwood. In 1769 Wedgwood acquired the lease of a house in Chelsea, where he set up his own decorating studios supervised by Rhodes under the direction of

Thomas Bentley. There in 1773-74 a group of artists employed by Wedgwood painted the 'Frog' service for Catherine the Great of Russia. It was completed in less than twelve months. This enormous service, the most prestigious ever made by Wedgwood, led the way in production of pottery and porcelain decorated with topographical painting, which became a distinct category referred to as 'Named Views.' To this category belong the American commemorative plates made from 1880 (Plates 35-37). Rococo shapes and decoration (Plates 53, 105) lingered until about 1775, but the majority of Josiah's tableware patterns were simple, elegant borders based on natural objects—foliage, flowers, fruit, seaweed or shells—or upon designs of respectable classical origins which suited neo-classical taste. (Plates 51, 52).

Some of Wedgwood's 18th century Queen's ware shapes, which combined beauty with function as they had seldom been combined before, have proved to be ageless and are still in production. The variety of these 'useful' wares is astonishing. They included not only all those pieces customarily associated with breakfast, dinner, tea and coffee services, but also such unusual objects as 'Egg Baskets to keep boiled eggs hot in water,' 'Monteiths for keeping Glasses cool in Water,' 'Strawberry Bowls,' 'Chestnut or Orange Baskets,' 'Ice Cream Cups,' 'Asparagus Pans,' and very large *Plats de Menage*, highly decorative centerpieces festooned with small baskets for sweetmeats. One of Josiah's earliest shapes was a 'Glacier' (Wedgwood's own and somewhat erratic name for a covered ice-pail), and creamware tiles, some hand-painted to match the ware made to furnish private dairies, were made as early as 1769. Some 2,000 shapes had been made by 1805, and many more have been added since that date.

Wedgwood's Queen's ware body has changed little in more than 200 years. The modern body is heavier and less brittle than its 18th century counterpart, and the glaze, once poisonous to workers who mixed and applied it, is now safe. The first of the stained clay colored bodies, *Celadon*, was introduced in 1805 and *Lavender* followed in 1850. *Honey-Buff* (1930), *Windsor Grey* (1953) and *Cane* (1957) are in the same tradition. In 1933 the first matte glazes were produced, and these were to be particularly important for the shapes designed by Keith Murray and figures by John Skeaping. The invention and development of glazes was also the special feature of Norman Wilson Unique Ware produced from 1932 to 1939 and from 1955 to 1963.

1. Cream-color pierced Chestnut or Orange basket, Shape No. 32 in the first Catalogue, 1774. This shape is still in production. Height 8 ins. Impressed WEDGWOOD. c. 1774

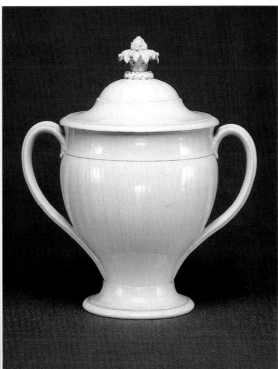

2. Three rare and early turned vases of deep cream color: two turned, with rouletted *guilloche* patterns on similar bases; and the third fluted, with molded lions' masks and floral swags. Height 13½ and 11½ ins. All unmarked. c. 1765

3. Cream-color cassolette or pot-pourri vase, fluted and turned, with rouletted pattern; and two *lignum vitae* roulettes, showing how the patterns were produced before the article was fired. Height 12½ ins. Unmarked. c. 1770

4. Cream-color engine-turned vase with elaborately built up leaf finial. Height 10 ins. Unmarked. c. 1770

5. Cream-color shell-edge teapot and covered jug, with interlaced handles and floral knobs, showing traces of gilding. Teapot height 6½ ins. Both impressed WEDGWOOD. c. 1770

6

7

6. Two cream-color Jelly molds, the one on the right molded with an Egyptian canopic figure. 8½ ins. by 6½ ins., and 7½ ins. by 6 ins. (oval). Unmarked. c. 1800

7. Cream-color egg-beater. The egg is broken into the base, the lid replaced, and the whole shaken, the projecting spikes blending yolk and white. Height 3⅞ ins. c. 1790

8. Cream-color stacking meat pans or food carriers. An early example of practical kitchenware. Height 14 ins. Impressed WEDGWOOD. c. 1850

9

44

9. Nereid Fruit Center. The finely modeled Nereid figures hold a fishing net, which forms the bowl, on a base of molded waves. Length 20 ins. Impressed WEDGWOOD. c. 1870

10. Imperial Queen's ware vase. An example of the finely pierced ornamental vases produced between 1860 and 1920. Height 10½ ins. Impressed WEDGWOOD. c. 1885

11

12

13

11. Melon teapot, height 5 ins., decorated with green and yellow glazes, with molded leaf spout and handle and flower knob. Unmarked. c. 1765

12. Cauliflower wares. Punch pot or Tea kettle, height 8 ins., coffeepot and cream boat, with leaf and cauliflower molding, decorated in green and yellow glazes. All unmarked. c. 1762

13. Green glaze candlestick, molded with overlapping leaves and owls' heads, the shape derived from silver. Height 11 ins. Unmarked. c. 1765

14

15

14. Two forms of pineapple teapots, one with hexagonal handle and spout, and both with pineapple knobs. Height 5 ins. Both unmarked. c. 1762

15. Ribbed vase, engine-turned, and decorated with green and brown glazes. Height 6¾ ins. Impressed **Wedgwood & Bentley**. c. 1775

16. Brown 'Rockingham' glazed jug, height 7 ins., with wheel engraved design cut through the glaze. No marks visible. c. 1877

18

17. Pear-shaped three-handled vase in cream-color, decorated with mingled green and brown glazes on a square black basalt plinth. Height 8¼ ins. WEDGWOOD & BENTLEY wafer mark. c. 1770

18. Cream color bulb, or hyacinth, pot with surface agate decoration. Height 7 ins. Impressed WEDGWOOD. c. 1785

19

20

19. Solid agate vase with cream-color hound handles. Height 6½ ins. Unmarked. c. 1761

20. Solid agate vase, Shape No. 1 in the Ornamental Shapes Book, with cream-color satyr-head handles, the horns piercing the rim of the neck. Square black basalt plinth. Height 12 ins. WEDGWOOD & BENTLEY wafer mark. c. 1770

21

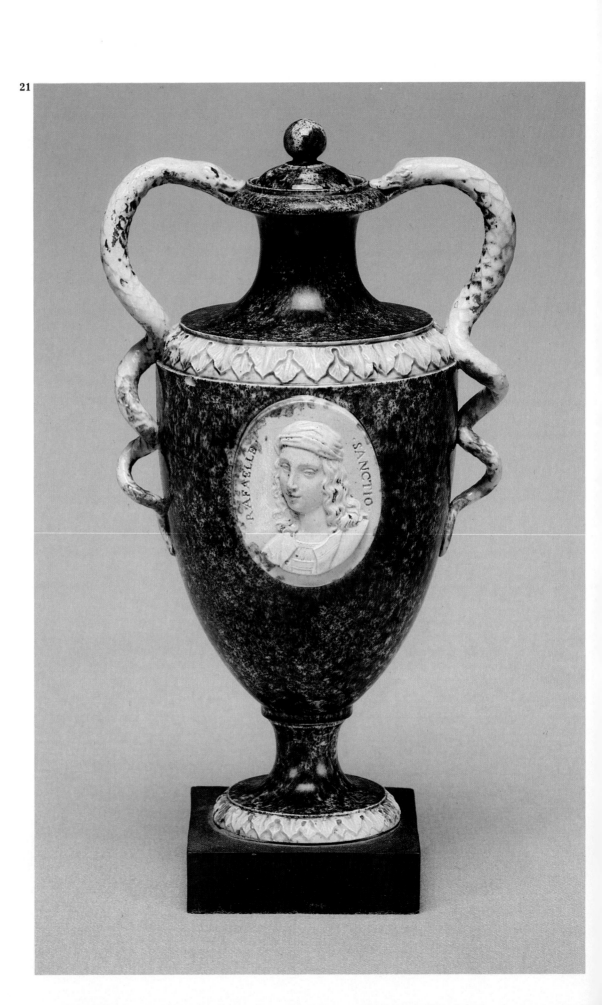

21. Cream color vase decorated with speckled blue and manganese glazes to resemble 'sprinkled porphyry.' Applied medallion of Raffaelle d'Urbino, and snake handles. Traces of gilding. Square black basalt base. Height 8½ ins. WEDGWOOD & BENTLEY wafer mark. c. 1774

22. Cream color ewer of Greek *oenochoe* shape with blue 'pebble' glaze, mask terminals to handle, and bands of overlapping leaves round the body. Traces of gilding. Square black basalt plinth. Height 13½ ins. WEDGWOOD & BENTLEY wafer mark. c. 1772

24

23. Funerary urn. Sprinkled porphyry decoration with flame knob
and applied leaves and swags.
Handles in the form of the heads
and shoulders of winged figures.
Height 20 ins. Impressed
WEDGWOOD. c. 1785

24. Two surface agate vases: (left)
Thrown and turned vase-candle-
stick with applied arabesque border
and leaves, and reversible cover
(for candlestick), square white
jasper plinth with key fret decoration and traces of gilding. Height 18
ins. Impressed WEDGWOOD. c. 1783;
(right) Snake-handled vase with applied acanthus leaf ornament at
neck and foot. Traces of gilding.
Height 14½ ins. Impressed
WEDGWOOD. c. 1775 (The impressed
plinth is of slightly later date)

25

26

58

25. D-shaped bulb pot ('root pot') decorated with brilliant mottled green ('Serpentine') glazes. Applied floral swags and acanthus border. Traces of gilding. Length 9½ ins. Impressed WEDGWOOD. c. 1785

26. Norman Wilson Unique Ware black and white marbled powder box, and two Norman Wilson trial marbled plates. Powder box, height 5 ins. Impressed WEDGWOOD NW. Plates diameter 10 ins. Unmarked. All c. 1955

27. Two Queen's ware dinner plates decorated with iron-red transfer-prints of birds by Sadler & Green: (left) Queen's shape, impressed WEDGWOOD; (right) Feather-edge, impressed WEDGWOOD. Diameter 9¾ ins. Both c. 1775

28. Queen's ware tankard decorated with Sadler & Green transfer print of a hunting scene. Height 6 ins. Impressed WEDGWOOD. c. 1770

29. Queen's ware tureen transfer-
printed in black with rural scenes
after engravings by Thomas Bewick
(1753-1828). Height 11 ins., diameter
14 ins. Impressed WEDGWOOD. c.
1777

30. Coffeepot decorated with Sadler
& Green transfer-print in red of
'Rural Lovers' after a painting by
Thomas Gainsborough (engraved
by Francis Vivares). Height 9¾ ins.
Impressed WEDGWOOD. c. 1775

31

32

31, 33. Queen's ware teapot decorated with Sadler & Green transfer-
prints of the Death of Wolfe from
the engraving by William Woollett
after Benjamin West, and 'Success
to the Independent Volunteer
Societies of the Kingdom of
Ireland.' Typical Wedgwood pierced ball knob and leafage spout.
Height 6½ ins. Impressed
WEDGWOOD. c. 1775

32. Queen's ware teapot decorated
with Sadler & Green transfer-print
of 'The Tea Party,' a popular print
which appeared, in various forms,
on the pottery and porcelain of
other manufacturers including
Worcester. The teapot has a split
handle with foliate terminals and a
rose knob and typical leafage (cabbage) spout. Height 5¼ ins. Impressed WEDGWOOD. c. 1775

34. Beane's Patent Tea Infuser. Queen's ware tea infuser, fitted with metal spigot, printed in red. Height 13½ ins. Impressed WEDGWOOD and illegible three-letter date mark, and printed inscription 'BEANES PATENT INFUSER.' c. 1880

35. Plate printed in red with view of the U.S. Military Academy. Commissioned by Jones, McDuffee & Stratton Co., 1936. Diameter 10½ ins. Impressed WEDGWOOD with printed WEDGWOOD ETRURIA ENGLAND, and special West Point backstamp

36. Plate printed in blue with view of the U.S. Naval Academy. Commissioned by Jones, McDuffee & Stratton Co., 1933. Diameter 10½ ins. Impressed WEDGWOOD with printed WEDGWOOD ETRURIA ENGLAND, and special backstamp

38

37. Oval dish, 17 ins. by 13½ ins. printed with view of Bowdoin College in black. Commissioned by Jones, McDuffee & Stratton Co., 1931. Impressed WEDGWOOD with printed WEDGWOOD ETRURIA ENGLAND, and descriptive backstamp. This, and the two previous illustrations are examples of the commemorative wares made from 1899 specially for the American market.

38. Plate printed in black with 'Ice Cutters,' one of the set of New England Industries designs by Claire Leighton, 1952. Diameter 10½ ins. Printed mark: WEDGWOOD OF ETRURIA & BARLASTON, MADE IN ENGLAND, descriptive backstamp, and facsimile signature of the artist.

40

39. Queen's ware bowl, diameter 12½ ins., printed in black with reproductions of engravings commemorating the signing of the Articles of Federation at Philadelphia on 9 July 1778. Designed by Alan Price, 1959. Impressed WEDGWOOD MADE IN ENGLAND, with special printed backstamp

40. Queen's ware jug, height 8 ins., printed in black with reproductions of engravings to commemorate the bicentennial of General James Wolfe's victory at Quebec in 1759. This piece makes an interesting comparison with the *Death of Wolfe* teapot (plates 31, 33) issued about 180 years earlier. Impressed WEDGWOOD MADE IN ENGLAND, with special commemorative printed backstamp

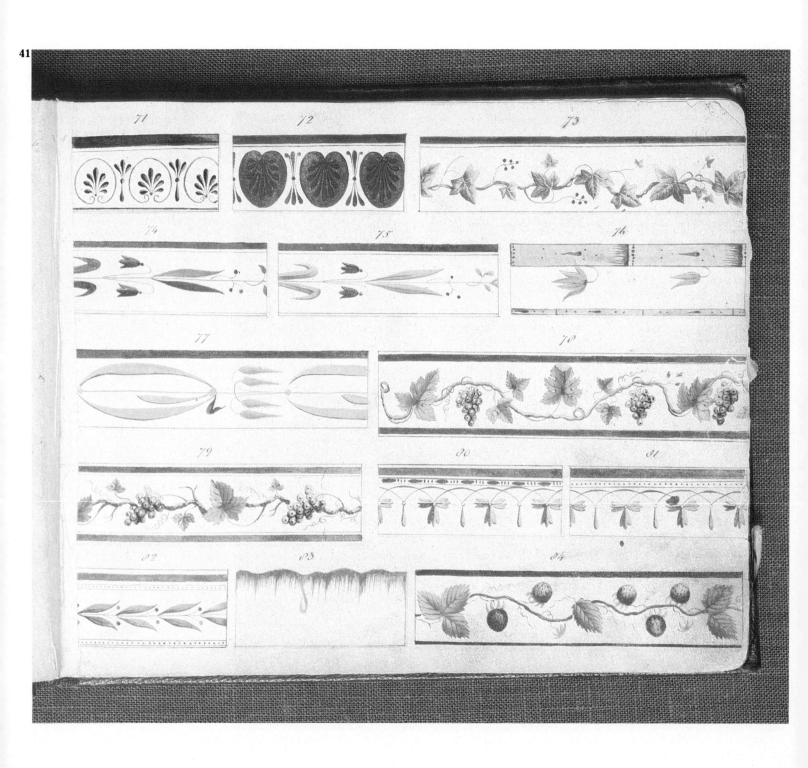

42

43

41. A page from the Wedgwood Queen's ware Pattern Book, a hand-painted record copied c. 1810 from the original started c. 1765

42. Lobed dish ('radish dish') shape no. 1318, painted in Puce with the *Husk* border and a flower center. 11½ ins. x 8½ ins. Impressed WEDGWOOD. c. 1765

43. Pierced Queen's ware plate painted in puce. Oval 10 ins. x 9 ins. Impressed WEDGWOOD. c. 1770

44

45

44. Queen's ware teapot of typical early Wedgwood shape, hand-painted with flowers. Height 5¾ ins. Impressed WEDGWOOD. c. 1768

45. Round dish, 11½ ins. diameter, painted at the Russian Poskotchin factory, probably as a replacement for a broken dish from the *Husk* service supplied to Catherine the Great in 1770. Impressed C II. Poskotchin factory, 1810

46. Queen's ware teapot, probably painted by David Rhodes, with typical pierced ball knob, and leafage spout and handle. Height 5¾ ins. Unmarked. c. 1765

47. Queen's ware teapot painted with a female figure of the type known as 'Miss Pit.' Similar teapots, of a slightly different shape, were made by the Leeds factory. Height 5¾ ins. Impressed WEDGWOOD. c. 1765

48

49

74

48. Two plates made for 'Catherine,' or 'Frog' service: (left) trial plate enameled in full color (a decoration found to be too expensive) and without the Frog emblem; (right) plate with a view of Ham House, showing the decoration as it was supplied. Both 8¾ ins. diameter. Unmarked. 1773-74

49. Oval dish from the same service, painted with a view of Kenilworth Castle. Oval length 12¼ ins. Impressed WEDGWOOD 1774.

50. Rare tankard enameled by David Rhodes. Height 5 ins. Unmarked. c. 1770

51

52

51. Queen's ware tureen painted with the anthemion pattern. Length 16½ ins. Impressed WEDGWOOD. c. 1770

52. Royal shape dish (originally modeled for George III), painted with 'Pink Antique' pattern. 17 ins. x 13 ins. Impressed WEDGWOOD. c. 1775

53. Extremely fine Queen's ware covered jug, painted with scenes of figures in landscapes, with painted rose knob and split, interlaced handles. Height 7¼ ins. Impressed WEDGWOOD. c. 1775

55

54. Two Queen's ware jugs, both made for Volunteer regimental officers: (left) painted with Masonic device on reverse; (right) painted with mounted cavalryman on reverse. Height 8 ins. Both impressed WEDGWOOD. c. 1786

55. Mustard pot, stand and spoon, painted in green. Height 3¾ ins. Impressed WEDGWOOD. c. 1770

56. 'Etruscan' pattern painted plate with center taken from an illustration of one of Sir William Hamilton's antique vases. Impressed WEDGWOOD. c. 1772

57

58

80

59

60

57. Circular painted tray, diameter 14½ ins. Impressed WEDGWOOD. c. 1785

58. Two tankards and a jug, painted with purple vine patterns. Tankards height 6½ ins.; jug height 6¾ ins. All impressed WEDGWOOD. c. 1775

59. 'Blue Weed' pattern painted plate, diameter 9¾ ins. Impressed WEDGWOOD. c. 1775

60. Plate painted with the arms of Honeywood and Courtenay. Impressed WEDGWOOD. c. 1775

61

62

63

Endsleigh Dairy.

61. Painted supper set in contemporary mahogany tray, diameter 13 ins. Trays impressed WEDGWOOD (pots unmarked). c. 1785

62. 'Bedford Grape' painted tureen, made for Lord William Russell at Woburn Abbey. Height 4½ ins., length 7½ ins. Impressed WEDGWOOD. c. 1815

63. Dairy cream vase made for the Endsleigh dairy owned by the Duke of Bedford. Height 16 ins. Impressed WEDGWOOD. c. 1822

64

65

64. Shaped dish, 9½ ins x 7 ins., painted with ivy pattern. This pattern may have been the prototype for the famous *Napoleon Ivy* (see plate 92). Impressed WEDGWOOD. c. 1790

65. Two painted Queen's ware jelly molds and covers. The plain covers were filled with jelly, and the painted interior shapes were placed inside them. When the jelly was set, the covers were removed, leaving the painted decoration to show through the transparent jelly. (Left) height 5¼ ins.; (right) height 8½ ins. without covers. Covers unmarked; interiors both impressed WEDGWOOD. c. 1785

66. Part of a painted Queen's ware set made for the Duke of Clarence and presented to the Stoke-on-Trent Museum by Queen Mary in 1913. Impressed WEDGWOOD. 1818

69

67. Shell-shaped dessert service, introduced c. 1790, with hand-painted border pattern. Large Nautilus shell 9 ins. high. All impressed WEDGWOOD. c. 1790

68. Fruit center painted with the *Lag & Feather* or *Flute & Wreath* pattern in brown and blue. Width 14 ins. Impressed WEDGWOOD. c. 1785

69. Parapet shape teapot decorated with *Agricultural Implements* in brown. Height 5½ ins. Impressed WEDGWOOD. c. 1820

70

71

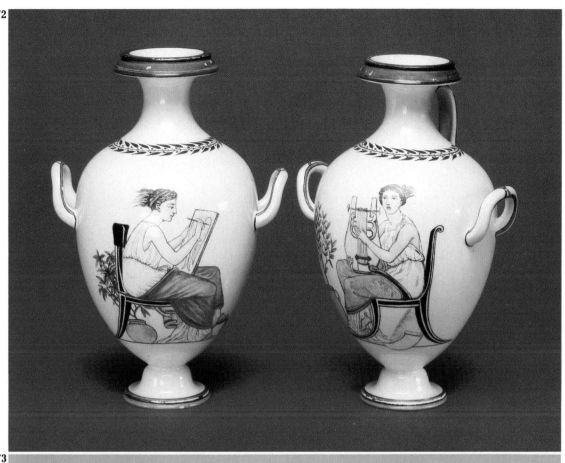

70. Shaped rectangular dish painted by Emile Lessore. 10½ ins. (corner to corner). Impressed WEDGWOOD. c. 1860

71. Pair of vases (shape no. 1) painted by Emile Lessore. Height 11¾ ins. Impressed WEDGWOOD. c. 1820

72. Pair of vases painted by Walter Crane (1845-1915) with figures of the arts of Music and Painting. Height 7¾ ins. Impressed WEDGWOOD WUQ. 1888

73. Inlaid teapot and candlesticks, the pattern incised and filled with contrasting slip before firing. Candlestick height 8½ ins. Impressed WEDGWOOD. c. 1870

74. 'Victoria ware' barbers bottles, enameled in blue with relief ornament and gilding. Vases of richly decorated Queen's ware were made by Wedgwood to compete with the porcelain vases of other manufacturers. Height 10½ ins. Impressed WEDGWOOD. c. 1860

75. Very rare inlaid and enameled vase by Thomas Mellor, height 15 ins. Impressed WEDGWOOD, and signed T. Mellor in script. c. 1880

77

78

76. Enameled and gilt busts of Mercury and Minerva, copied from 18th century originals first produced in black basalt. Heights 21¼ ins. and 22 ins. Impressed WEDGWOOD MERCURY and WEDGWOOD MINERVA. c. 1900

77. 'Victoria ware' salmon-ground vases with relief ornament and richly gilt. Height 5½ ins. Impressed WEDGWOOD. c. 1860

78. Dish decorated by Charles Passenger, a partner of William De Morgan (1839-1917), with typical De Morgan crimson lustre. Impressed WEDGWOOD, and signed with Passenger's monogram on the base. 9 ins. diameter. c. 1885

79. Vase, painted and signed by Christopher Dresser (1834-1904). Impressed WEDGWOOD. Height 10¼ ins. c. 1895

80. Plaque, 15 ins. diameter, painted by Thomas Allen (1831-1915), Wedgwood's art director from 1876 until his retirement in 1905, with a portrait of Falstaff on a rich gold ground. Impressed WEDGWOOD. 1881

81. Oval tray, 16¾ ins. x 11¼ ins., painted with purple vine pattern. Impressed WEDGWOOD 3LK. 1908. This piece is an interesting example of the quality of Wedgwood's freehand painting, and reproduction of early patterns, in the 20th century

82. Vase painted by Lindsay Butterfield (1869-1948). Height 8¼ ins. Impressed WEDGWOOD, with printed mark 'Lindsay' in script and special backstamp. c. 1910

83. Superb round dish, or charger, painted by Alfred Powell, who joined Wedgwood with his wife, Louise, in 1905, and founded a new school of freehand painting at Etruria. Diameter 18½ ins. Impressed WEDGWOOD 455 and painted Alfred Powell mongram. c. 1920

84. Large circular wall plaque (pierced for hanging) painted in purple lustre with a view of Barlaston Hall by Alfred Powell. Powell's monogram appears in platinum on the reverse, with the painted inscription, 'Alfred Powell at Barlaston May 1942'. 23 ins. diameter

85

86

85. 'Boat Race' bowl designed by Eric Ravilious (1903-42) to commemorate the Oxford and Cambridge boat race of 1938. Black print and polychrome enamel on Queen's ware. Diameter 12¼ ins. Black printed backstamp including 'WEDGWOOD MADE IN ENGLAND.' 1938

86. Dinner plate and dessert plate in the *Travel* and *Persephone* patterns designed by Eric Ravilious in 1938. The *Travel* pattern was not produced until after the death of the artist in action in the 1939-45 War. *Persephone,* also enameled in green and yellow, was reproduced in 1953. Impressed marks WEDGWOOD MADE IN ENGLAND and descriptive backstamps. Diameter 10 ins. 1953

87. *Garden Implements* jug and beakers designed by Eric Ravilious in 1938. Jug height 7½ ins. Impressed WEDGWOOD MADE IN ENGLAND with printed backstamp

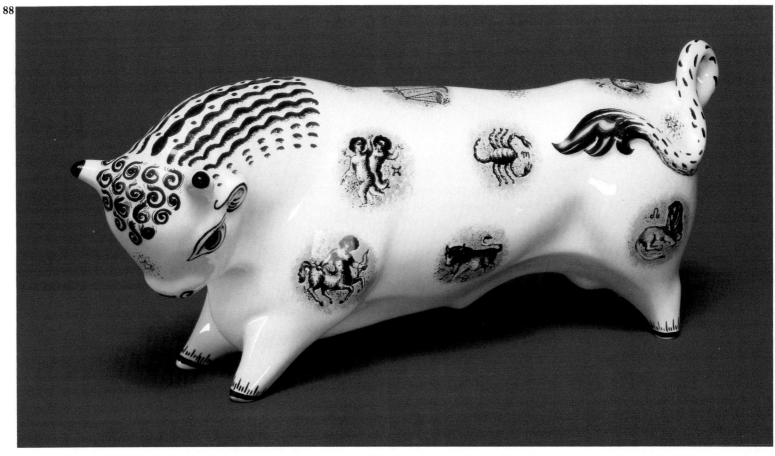

88. Model of Taurus the Bull by Arnold Machin RA (b. 1911) decorated with Signs of the Zodiac designed by Eric Ravilious. Length 14 ins. This model was also produced with the floral *Avon* pattern decoration. Impressed WEDGWOOD MADE IN ENGLAND AM, with printed mark WEDGWOOD BARLASTON ENGLAND. 1945

89. 'Country Lovers' modeled by Arnold Machin RA. Height 13 ins. Circular printed backstamp WEDGWOOD OF ETRURIA & BARLASTON. 1945

90. 'Bridal Group' designed by Arnold Machin RA, 1941. This group admirably illustrates Machin's earthy sense of humor: the bride's condition has evidently accelerated the marriage, and the page has forgotten his handkerchief. 11½ ins. high x 10 ins. wide. Impressed WEDGWOOD MADE IN ENGLAND, with printed backstamp

91. 'Thrower' modeled by Arnold Machin RA. A fine and rare figure illustrating one of the most important of pottery crafts. Height 11 ins. Impressed WEDGWOOD MADE IN ENGLAND, with printed backstamp

92. *Napoleon Ivy* punch bowl, diameter 11¾ ins., height 6¾ ins. Backstamped 'NAPOLEON IVY AS USED BY NAPOLEON AT ST. HELENA 1815. WEDGWOOD OF ETRURIA & BARLASTON.' 1953

93. A selection of Queen's ware mugs: (left to right) ABC mug by Eric Ravilious; mug designed by Eric Ravilious for the Coronation of Edward VIII and reproduced for the Coronations of George VI (illustrated) and Queen Elizabeth II (pink and yellow); Festival of Britain mug designed by Norman Mackinson 1951; and Barlaston mug designed by Ravilious to commemorate the founding of the Barlaston factory 1938. Larger mugs height 4½ ins.

94. A selection of commemorative mugs, height 4½ ins., designed by Richard Guyatt: (left to right) American Bicentennial mug 1976; Silver Jubilee mug 1977; drab ware Silver Wedding mug 1974; Coronation mug 1953; and Prince of Wales Investiture mug 1969. All marked with special commemorative backstamps

107

95

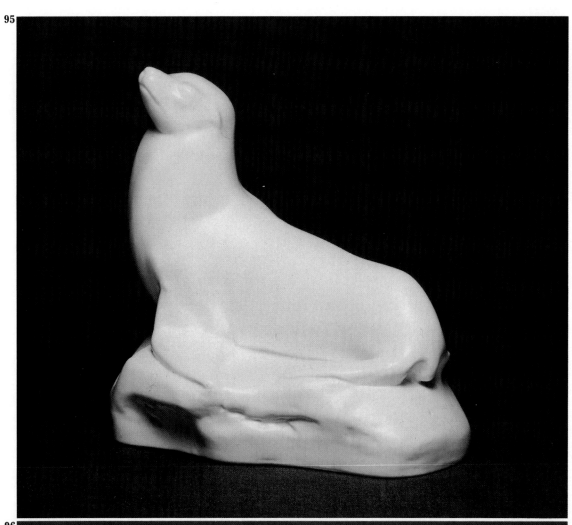

96

95. 'Sea Lion' modeled by John Skeaping RA (b. 1901) and decorated with Moonstone glaze. Skeaping modeled a number of animals for Wedgwood, all of which became popular decorated in matte colored glazes developed by Norman Wilson. Height 11 ins. Printed mark in green 'WEDGWOOD BARLASTON ENGLAND.' 1953

96. Jug and one-pint mug of Celadon and cream-color slipware designed by Keith Murray (b. 1892) in 1935. The creamware is dipped in Celadon slip and the three lines are cut on the lathe before firing. Jug height 8½ ins. Impressed WEDGWOOD MADE IN ENGLAND with special circular backstamp (mug marked with backstamp only). 1955

97. 'Standing Duiker' modeled by John Skeaping RA and decorated with Champagne glaze. Height 7½ ins. Impressed WEDGWOOD MADE IN ENGLAND. c. 1930

98. 'Annular' shaped vase covered with matte green glaze, designed by Keith Murray in 1935. This illustrates Murray's use of the lathe to produce shapes in keeping with Art Déco taste of the period. Impressed WEDGWOOD MADE IN ENGLAND: incised Keith Murray (facsimile signature). Height 9 ins.

99. Toby Jug, cream-color covered with amber glaze. Wedgwood's only figure of this well-known type, representing Elihu Yale, benefactor of Yale University. Inscribed on the base: THE ELIHU YALE TOBY, Patent applied for, RGE Sculp, 1938 WEDGWOOD MADE IN ENGLAND. 6⅜ ins. height

100. 'Springtime' vase by Keith Murray decorated, over Moonstone matte glaze, with hand-painted floral spray by Millicent Taplin. Height 8 ins. Printed mark: KM WEDGWOOD MADE IN ENGLAND (no impressed mark) c. 1940

101

102

101. Aventurine glaze bowl designed by Norman Wilson for his range of Unique Ware. Diameter 5¼ ins. Impressed WEDGWOOD MADE IN ENGLAND NW. 1954

102. Turquoise glaze and platinum painted bowl designed by Norman Wilson and painted by Millicent Taplin. Diameter 8 ins.; height 2½ ins. Impressed WEDGWOOD MADE IN ENGLAND and printed mark WEDGWOOD NW in gray. 1953

103. Vase of Chinese form decorated in brilliant white and mottled blue glazes. One of the range of Norman Wilson Unique Ware pieces designed between 1932 and 1963. Height 8 ins. Printed mark WEDGWOOD NW in green. Impressed WEDGWOOD NW. c. 1953

Pearl

Wedgwood's pursuit of a white tableware, for which influential patrons often asked him, led him to introduce in 1779, a new body similar to Queen's ware but containing a larger proportion of white clay and flint. The glaze had a small quantity of cobalt oxide added, further to whiten the appearance of the body. 'Pearl,' as he named the new body, was used in Josiah I's time principally for the production of patterns hand-painted in underglaze blue (Plate 105), which tended to take on a green tinge on creamware, but some fine enameled jugs were also produced (Plates 107-108) which became an important part of Wedgwood's production in the 19th century. From 1805, however, it was the essential ground for underglaze blue printed patterns (Plates 114-116). From about 1830, the number of topographical or invented landscape patterns increased, but centers that were clearly Oriental in inspiration were teamed with unashamedly English floral borders. The mixture of styles is curiously satisfying.

Pearl was also the body principally used for lustre decoration, introduced in 1806. Wedgwood's variegated and marbled lustres, produced by the use of oxides of such metals as gold and platinum, were distinctive, and examples are now rare (Plates 109-110). Towards the end of the century William de Morgan rediscovered the secret of the red and purple lustres produced 300 years earlier in Italy, and both he and his partner, Charles Passenger, decorated ware produced by Wedgwood. At about the same time, Pearl ware was also used for some mildly eccentric photolithographic reproductions of scenes of stags in the Scottish Highlands, drawn by a retired army general (Page 17). Pearl ware was produced by other manufacturers, notably Spode. It has not been made by Wedgwood since 1940.

104

105

104. Pair of rococo shell compotiers, the edges painted in underglaze blue. Width 7½ ins. Impressed WEDGWOOD. c. 1780

105. Sauce tureen and stand, shell-edge shape, with underglaze blue painted 'Mared' (Onion) pattern and enameled edges, the finial in the shape of a sea horse, on fixed stand. Length of stand 10 ins. Impressed WEDGWOOD. c. 1782

106. Shell shaped compotier, painted in black and enameled in bright green by Sadler & Green, Liverpool, for Wedgwood c. 1780. Wedgwood's interest in shells led him to introduce essentially rococo shapes into many of his designs

06

107

108

107. Jug painted with a spray of naturalistic flowers, the reverse with a bunch of white grapes, and monogram and date 1797 below the lip. Height 7¾ ins. Impressed WEDGWOOD

108. Jug, printed and enameled with 'The Farmers Arms' and 'Spring' (reverse). Height 8 ins. Impressed WEDGWOOD. c. 1790

THE FARMERS ARMS

IN GOD IS OUR TRUST

109

110

111

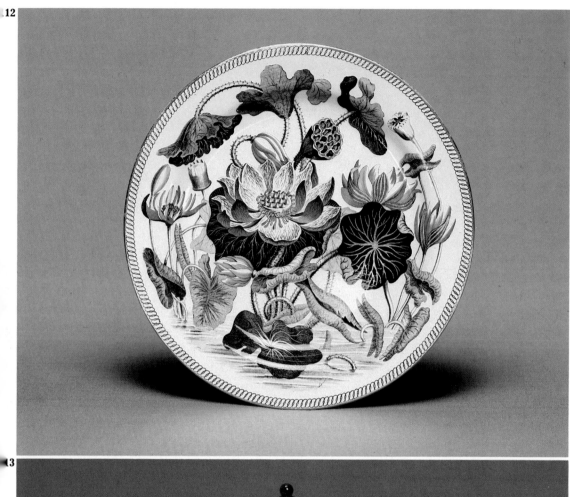

109. Variegated, or 'marbled' lustre cup and saucer and jug, the delicate shades of color and lustre reflection produced by the use of oxides of iron, platinum and gold. Jug height 5½ ins. Impressed WEDGWOOD. c. 1810

110. Variegated lustre ('marbled lustre') shell wall pocket and dessert plate. Wall pocket 9½ ins. wide, 6 ins. high. Impressed WEDGWOOD. c. 1810

111. Plain Pearl parapet shape teapot finished with a simple gold line and lightly gilded knob. Compare with bone china teapot illustrated at plate 284. Impressed WEDGWOOD. c. 1820

112. Brown *Water Lily* pattern plate with 'botanical' border. First produced in 1808 and sometimes erroneously called the 'Darwin Water Lily.' Diameter 9¾ ins. Impressed WEDGWOOD

113. Garniture of two bough pots and a cassolette vase, decorated with very dark brown slip, engine-turned, diced and ornamented with applied swags. The bough pots have plain pierced Pearl ware lids. Impressed WEDGWOOD. Heights 11 ins. and 7½ ins. c. 1790

114

115

116

114. Underglaze blue printed *Bamboo* pattern soup plate, diameter 9¾ ins. Impressed WEDGWOOD. c. 1806

115. Underglaze blue printed *Water Lily* pattern mug and jug with 'cut reed' border (Cf. plate 112). The most distinguished and original of all Wedgwood blue-printed patterns, the underglaze blue *Water Lily* was introduced in 1811. Mug height 5 ins. Jug height 9½ ins. Impressed WEDGWOOD

116. Underglaze blue printed *Hibiscus* pattern plate, diameter 9¾ ins. Impressed WEDGWOOD. c. 1807

117. Bourdalou (coach pot) decorated with underglaze blue prints of landscapes and rose border. Length 10½ ins. The bourdalou was a small chamber pot for female use, said to be named after a preacher at the Court of Louis XIV whose sermons were uncomfortably long. Impressed WEDGWOOD. c. 1830

117

118

119

118. Bulb pot (for hyacinths and crocuses) made as part of a set to celebrate the Golden Jubilee of George III in 1810. The decoration is a stippled orange ground print, a print of the Garter badge, and enameled flowers in the *famille rose* style. Height 6 ins. Impressed WEDGWOOD on pot and stand

119. Derby style tea service with underglaze blue panels and Oriental style flowers. Teapot 8½ ins. wide, 4½ ins. high. All impressed WEDGWOOD. c. 1810

120. *Chrysanthemum ('Cryxa')* pattern tea service decorated with stippled ground print and enameled floriate pattern in the Japanese style. Teapot 9¼ ins. wide, 4 ins. high. All except one saucer impressed WEDGWOOD. First introduced 1808

121. Another version of the *Cryxa* pattern on a shaped rectangular compotier heightened with gold. 9½ ins. x 8½ ins. Impressed WEDGWOOD. c. 1810

123

122. Printed and enameled plate, diameter 9 ins. Impressed WEDGWOOD ETRURIA. c. 1840

123. (Left) Plate with printed blue ground and enameled flowers. Impressed WEDGWOOD. c. 1812; (right) Plate with blue groundlaid enamel border and painted flowers and leaves. 9¼ ins. x 8 ins. diameter Impressed WEDGWOOD. c. 1815

Majolica

I talian *maiolica*, a reddish earthenware covered with glaze made white and opaque by the addition of tin oxide, and particularly noted for the quality of its polychrome enamel decoration, has little but its name to connect it with the Majolica produced by English pottery manufacturers during the second half of the 19th century. The latter is an 'art pottery,' decorated with opaque or transparent glazes, and appears to have been inspired by the 16th century pottery of Bernard Palissy, who spent many years trying to discover the secret of Italian *maiolica* and produced, instead, colored-glazed ware. English majolica was introduced at Minton's by Léon Arnoux in 1850, at a time when Palissy ware was greatly in demand among collectors. Wedgwood's majolica was first produced in 1860 (though by strict definition the early green glazed wares might be included in this category) and consisted of colored glazes applied over an earthenware body molded with relief ornament. Among ware of this type, which included some very large pieces more than 50 inches in height, were vases, *jardinières,* umbrella stands, wall brackets, candlesticks, comports, and dessert plates (Plates 124-130), Plates decorated by the so-called *émail ombrant* technique (Plate 131) are also in this category. Production of Wedgwood majolica ceased in 1910, and it was, for many years, neglected by succeeding generations who did not admire its rather florid appearance. Recently, however, collectors have begun to appreciate its quality and to understand its importance as an expression of Victorian taste.

124

124. (Left) Leaf-molded dessert plate decorated with mingled green and brown glazes, closely related to the glazes developed by the first Josiah a hundred years earlier. Impressed WEDGWOOD. 1860. (right) Dessert plate molded in the form of a sunflower, a favorite motif of the Aesthetic movement of the 1880s, and decorated with colored glazes. Diameter 8½ ins. Impressed WEDGWOOD. c. 1875

125. Jug, or *Stein,* with pewter lid, the body based on a German stoneware shape, molded with the inscription 'WHAT THO' MY GATES BE POOR/TAKE THEM IN GOOD PART/BETTER CHEER YOU MAY HAVE/BUT NOT WITH BETTER HEART.' Texts of such an improving nature were much favored at this period. Height 10 ins. Impressed WEDGWOOD CGY and Registry mark for 1867. 1870

126

127

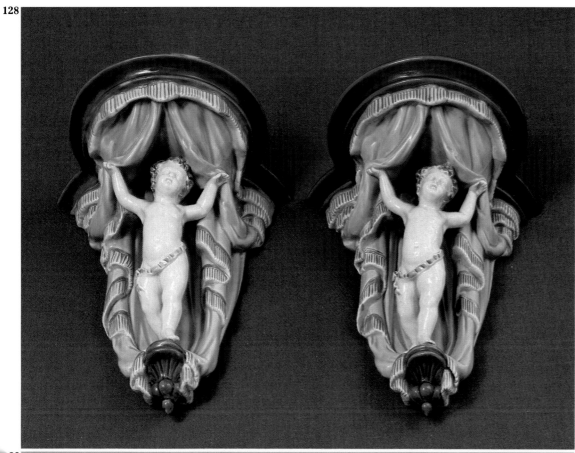

128

126. Jug decorated with overlapping vine leaves and bunches of grapes, decorated with colored glazes. Height 6½ ins. Printed WEDGWOOD ETRURIA ENGLAND. c. 1892

127. Pair of Dolphin candlesticks, from 18th century models sometimes attributed to Josiah I, decorated with colored glazes. Height 9½ ins. Impressed WEDGWOOD. c. 1860

128. Pair of wall brackets, height 9 ins., decorated with colored glazes. Impressed WEDGWOOD YZW. 1868

129. Strawberry dish formed in the shape of the fruit and molded with strawberry leaves and flowers, decorated with opaque and semi-transparent glazes. Length 10 ins. Impressed WEDGWOOD MAB. 1873

129

131

130. Molded dessert plates covered with opaque white glaze and decorated in enamel by Emile Lessore. Diameter 9½ ins. and 9 ins. Impressed WEDGWOOD FNU and WEDGWOOD FOT. 1866 and 1865

131. Molded octagonal dessert plate decorated in the manner known as *émail ombrant*. The deep intaglio molding, flooded with semi-transparent glaze, reveals the center relief design. This process was acquired under license by Wedgwood in 1873. Width 9¼ ins. Impressed WEDGWOOD OSZ. 1897

132. Large jardinière modeled by Hugues Protât and decorated with colored glazes. The shape is in the Sèvres style and the panels are painted by Emile Lessore. Oval 17 ins. x 10½ ins., height 8¾ ins. Impressed WEDGWOOD NQZ. 1871

133. Large ewer designed by Hugues Protât, decorated with colored glazes and paintings by Emile Lessore. Height 15 ins. Impressed WEDGWOOD.c. 1865

II. Stoneware
(Dry Bodies)

Black Basalt

Wedgwood's black basalt was perfected in 1768. A black earthenware known as 'Black Egyptian' had been made in Staffordshire for many years, but Wedgwood's hard, dense 'black porcelaine,' which he named after the natural stone used in ancient Egypt for sculpture, was so great a refinement upon earlier wares as to be almost a new invention. He described it as "having nearly the same properties as the Basalt [natural stone], resisting the Attacks of Acid; being a Touchstone to Copper, Silver and Gold; admitting of a good polish (if desired, by lapidary techniques); and capable of bearing to be made red hot in a furnace frequently without damage."

Basalt was clearly a body suitable for engine-turned decoration and cast ornament (the technique of applying sprigged ornament was to take some years to perfect) and within a year Josiah had taken out a patent for 'encaustic' painting in enamel. This technique was inspired by the ancient Greek and Italian red-figure vases, and the source of many of Wedgwood's designs was Sir William Hamilton's collection sold in 1772 to the British Museum. The colors, the surface of which is matte, are smooth and durable, and they were applied in the usual way with a brush. The palette was limited, red and white predominating, but green and blue were used, and almost a full range of colors appears on exceptionally rare tablets intended to be set into chimney-pieces. Probably the most celebrated of the encaustic painted vases are the 'First Day's Vases' thrown by Josiah with Bentley's help on 13 June 1769 to commemorate the founding of the Etruria factory (Plate 134).

The range of wares produced in black basalt included vases, bowls, flower pots, bulb pots, plaques, tablets, medallions, library busts, figures, portrait medallions, cameos, intaglio seals candlesticks, lamps, inkstands, kettles, and tea and coffee sets. Early difficulties in applying relief ornament were overcome, casts and models of sculpture and metalwork by famous artists were obtained from leading makers of plaster casts, and modelers were employed or trained at Etruria. The demand for basalt, particularly for vases, appeared to be insatiable, and it continued throughout the 18th century. Production has never totally ceased, although the popularity of basalt has varied according to fashion. In 1810, enameled decoration in the *famille rose* style was introduced and a little later more naturalistic flower and leaf patterns appeared (Plate 161). Library busts were again popular in the mid-19th century, and the sculptor, E.W. Wyon, supplied original models of eminent Victorians. To the 1880s belong the traditional basalt vase shapes ornamented with bronze and gold classical reliefs (Plate 164) and the brown ('bronze') basalt ornamented in gold. Both owed something to the interest in Japanese bronzes at that time. The period of production was short, probably because the mixture of styles was too bizarre even for Victorian taste.

Among the most important pieces introduced in the 20th century are Arnold Machin's *Taurus* (also, glazed with gold print decoration by Ravilious), bowls designed by Keith Murray, and the coffee set by Robert Minkin (Plate 165).

134. Front and reverse of First Day's Vase, thrown by Josiah Wedgwood while his partner, Thomas Bentley turned the wheel, on June 13 1769 to inaugurate the Etruria factory. Height 10 ins. Unmarked

135

144

135. Bust of William Shakespeare, first issued in black basalt in 1774. Height 19 ins. Impressed WEDGWOOD & BENTLEY SHAKESPEARE. c. 1775

136. Encaustic painted cream jug and teacup and saucer. Creamer 3½ ins. high. Teacup and saucer impressed WEDGWOOD; creamer impressed WEDGWOOD & BENTLEY. The use of the Wedgwood & Bentley mark on the creamer may have been in error, or perhaps to indicate that the piece was to be considered as a 'Cabinet' piece, and therefore ornamental and within the Wedgwood, Wedgwood & Bentley partnership. c. 1772

137. Framed plaque, 'Herculaneum Dancer,' diameter 15 ins. One of the set of 14 Herculaneum subjects molded directly from a set of casts in the Marquess of Lansdowne's possession c. 1772 and reproduced in black basalt, terracotta, and jasper with matching frames, some of which were gilded. The basalt plaques were frequently provided with red encaustic-painted backgrounds. Unmarked. c. 1774. Framed pieces of this type were almost always unmarked since they were intended for setting into the wall.

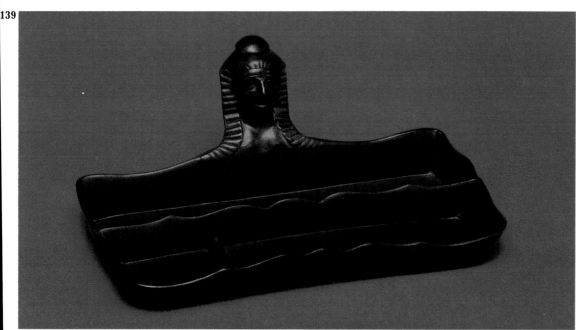

139

40

138. Framed plaque ornamented with a figure of the philosopher Zeno on encaustic painted ground. Oval 14 ins. x 12 ins. Unmarked. c. 1772

139. Egyptian style Sphinx-head ink stand and pen tray, 7½ ins. x 4½ ins. Very rare Wedgwood & Bentley mark in script. c. 1770

140. Rum kettle with molded relief of 'Boys bringing home the Game,' engine-turned lid, and bail handle. Height 10¾ ins. Unmarked. c. 1772

141. Pair of engine-turned vases with leopard's head handles. Height 17 ins. WEDGWOOD & BENTLEY wafer mark. c. 1775

142. Memorial vase to Henry Earle, the shape similar to that of the First Days vase, encaustic painted in white and green, and inscribed 'MEMORIAE S HENRICI EARLE VIXIT ANNOS LXI MORT: IAN DIE XXXI AD MDCCLXXIII.' Height 14¾ ins. Unmarked. 1774

143. Encaustic painted Canopic jar, height 12¾ ins. The Egyptian taste was very sophisticated in the 18th century and only became widely popular after Napoleon's invasion of Egypt and Nelson's victory at the Nile in 1798. Unmarked. c. 1775

144. Figure of Jean-Jacques Rousseau, modeled by William Hackwood in 1779 as the pair to one of Voltaire. It was also made in the Cane body, but examples in either body are rare. Height 11¾ ins. Impressed WEDGWOOD. c. 1780

145

146

145. Oval plaque, 'The Frightened Horse,' modeled by George Stubbs RA, c. 1780. 14¼ ins. by 8¾ ins. Inscribed WEDGWOOD. Modern reproduction. 1973

146. Figure of a Sleeping Boy (sometimes erroneously described as 'Somnus'); one of a series of five models first produced in basalt in 1773 after originals by Duquesnoy ('Il Fiammingo'). Length 5¼ ins. Unmarked. c. 1775

147. Pair of Wine and Water ewers. The Water ewer has the figure of a Triton seated on the shoulder, clasping the neck, and the Wine ewer a Satyr in the same position. These models were supplied by Flaxman in 1775. Jasper models are extremely rare, but versions also exist in bone china and Majolica. Height 16 ins. WEDGWOOD & BENTLEY. c. 1778

148

149

154

148. Extremely rare turned saucer dish with incised center decoration of formalized flower head. Diameter 7¾ ins. Impressed WEDGWOOD. c. 1785

149. Silver mounted cylindrical engine-turned tankard, height 5½ ins., molded in relief with 'Boys bringing home the Game' ('Boys returning from the Hunt'). Impressed Wedgwood. c. 1785

150. Bulb, or hyacinth, pot, height 5¾ ins., painted in red and white encaustic colors, with applied ornament of Cupids with Wreath. Impressed WEDGWOOD. c. 1800

151. Flared engine-turned spittoon. Height 3½ ins., diameter 4¾ ins. Impressed Wedgwood. c. 1785

152

153

152. Kylix, with double loop handles, encaustic painted with red and white palmettes. Height 8 ins., diameter 14 ins. Impressed WEDGWOOD. c. 1785

153. Pair of tripod vase-candlesticks with reversible lids, one end forming the socket for a candlestick. Such dual-purpose pieces were extremely popular, and several of Wedgwood's 18th century models for basalt and jasper were designed for more than one use. Height 9½ ins. (11½ ins. as candlesticks). Impressed Wedgwood. c. 1785

154. Encaustic painted leopards' head handle vase with Sibyl or 'Widow' knob (the widow with unusual encaustic painted face, hands and feet). Height 15 ins. Impressed WEDGWOOD. c. 1785

155. Griffin (or gryphon) bronzed candlestick, believed to have been modeled by Josiah I with the aid of Thomas Boot, a modeler at Etruria. The rare green patination, simulating old bronze, was produced by applying pure gold dissolved in *aqua regia* (a mixture of nitric and hydrochloric acids) with bronze filings. Height 13½ ins. Impressed WEDGWOOD. c. 1785

156. The so-called Michelangelo Vase ('Michelangelo Lamp') in the form of a large covered bowl with three burners on a column and pedestal support. The palm finial is surrounded by three Sibyl, or widow, figures, and the bowl is supported by three stooping male figures which derive from a crucifix by Antonio Gentile da Faenza (1531-1609), believed by Sir William Chambers to have been modeled originally by Michelangelo Buonarotti. Height 13 ins. Impressed WEDGWOOD. c. 1785

157. Simple engine-turned covered jug with split handle. Height 9 ins. Impressed WEDGWOOD. c. 1780

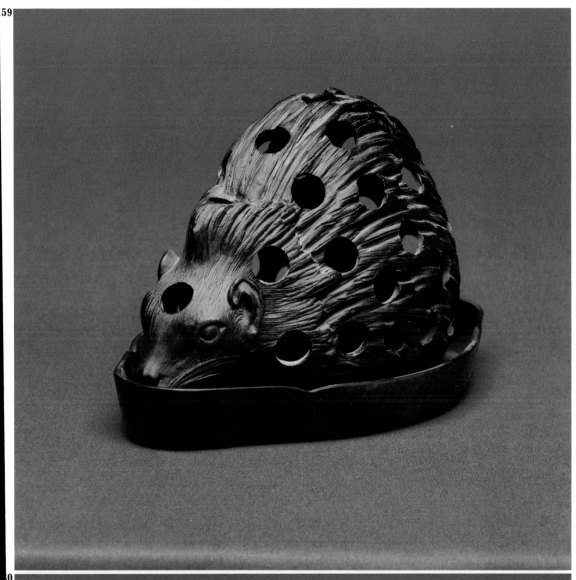

158. Fine bust of Mercury, modeled by John Flaxman RA in 1782. Height 18½ ins. Another similar bust was refinished by Hackwood in 1779 from a cast supplied by Hoskins & Grant. Impressed WEDGWOOD. c. 1785

159. Hedgehog crocus pot and stand. The hedgehog was filled with moss or soil, placed on the tray base, and then planted with crocuses which grew through the holes in its back. The same model was later made in green glazed creamware and the Lavender body. Height 7 ins.; tray length 11 ins. Impressed WEDGWOOD on tail, c. 1785, the later base impressed WEDGWOOD MADE IN ENGLAND indicating a date after 1898

160. Canopic inkstand ornamented with 'Egyptian' reliefs in rosso antico. Length 12 ins., height 5¼ ins. The model is an odd mixture of Greek and Egyptian motifs which might be called 'Classicized Egyptian.' Impressed WEDGWOOD. c. 1805

161. Floral painted and engine-turned déjeuner or Early Morning Teaset, comprising teapot, sugar box, creamer, teacup and saucer, bowl and oval tray, enameled in green, yellow, blue and pink. Tray (unmarked) length 14 ins. All other pieces impressed WEDGWOOD. c. 1815

162. King and Queen from the chess set designed by Arnold Machin RA in 1939. Sets were made in black basalt and blue jasper, and lavender and cream-color Queen's ware. Height of King 5¼ ins. Impressed WEDGWOOD AM MADE IN ENGLAND. 1939

163. Silver Wedding mug designed by Richard Guyatt in 1972 to commemorate the 25th Wedding Anniversary of H.M. Queen Elizabeth II. Impressed WEDGWOOD MADE IN ENGLAND 72 and printed with special backstamp. Height 4¼ ins.

164. Basalt vase with relief ornament decorated with bronze and gold. This type of decoration, influenced by the fashion for Japanese bronzes, was produced for a short period from c. 1880. Height 12 ins. Impressed WEDGWOOD. c. 1885

165. Cylindrical coffeepot, sugar box and creamer designed by Robert Minkin, Wedgwood's Art Director from 1979. Coffeepot height 9 ins. Impressed WEDGWOOD MADE IN ENGLAND. 1963

166. Canopic vase with terracotta jasper hieroglyph reliefs, adapted from an 18th century original. Impressed WEDGWOOD MADE IN ENGLAND 78. Height 9½ ins.

168

167. Gilded basalt plaque, 'Lord of the Diadems,' from the 'Egyptian Collection' produced in 1976. 8¾ ins. by 8 ins. Impressed WEDGWOOD MADE IN ENGLAND 76 and printed with special backstamp in gold

168. Gilded Sphinx figure adapted for the 'Egyptian Collection' from an 18th century model. Height 9 ins. Impressed WEDGWOOD MADE IN ENGLAND 78

Cane

First produced in 1770, cane ware is tan-colored stoneware produced by refining the local clays used by Staffordshire potters for traditional brown wares. It varied in color from a rich tan-yellow to buff, the darker shades being used for 'Bamboo' (Plates 169-173) in imitation of earlier Chinese wares. The earliest cane ware was, according to Josiah's high standards, "very imperfect. It has a coarse speckled appearance if examin'd with attention." The body was refined after 1783 and became, next to jasper and basalt, Wedgwood's most important ornamental body, besides being used for a variety of 'useful' wares. It was decorated in many ways: by engine-turning, encaustic painting, enameling, and cast or sprigged relief ornament, sometimes in contrasting color. Some rare examples were gilded (Plate 175). A coarser cane body was used from about 1798 for the production of game-pie dishes (Plate 174) and other pastry ware. From about 1815, smear-glaze was used on cane ware. This was presumably a decorative addition, since cane is a stoneware which needs glazing only to prevent staining.

Cane was copied in the 18th and 19th centuries, notably by the Spode, Davenport, Liverpool Herculaneum, Elijah Mayer and Turner factories. In the 20th century its previous popularity inspired the production of tableware in stained Queen's ware *(Honey-Buff, Cane* and *Harvest Moon)* and Primrose jasper (1976).

169

169. Footed bowl, cover and stand decorated with blue and white encaustic colors in the cut bamboo pattern. The bowl, cover and stand are molded in bamboo shapes. Height 5¼ ins. Impressed WEDGWOOD. c. 1785

170. Two-handled candlestick-vase-bough pot molded to simulate bamboo, the rim painted with a broad blue band, and the whole painted with green leaves and flowers in encaustic colors. Height 8 ins. Impressed WEDGWOOD HZ. c. 1785

172

173

171. Silver-mounted caneware tankard, the handle and base molded with bamboo shapes, and the rim glazed and painted with tongue pattern in blue. The interior of the tankard is glazed, and the body molded in relief with 'Boys returning from the Hunt' ('Boys bringing home the Game'). Height 10 ins. Impressed Wedgwood. c. 1785

172. Déjeuner or Early Morning Teaset molded to simulate bamboo, with matching handles and spouts, and encaustic enamel border decoration of blue and white laurel leaves on a broad terracotta colored band. Impressed WEDGWOOD Z (Teapot and sugar box); WEDGWOOD 2 (cup & saucer). 11 ins. x 9¼ ins. c. 1782

173. Hyacinth pot molded to simulate bamboo and decorated in green and black encaustic colors with bamboo leaves and cut bamboo pattern. Height 8½ ins. Impressed WEDGWOOD. c. 1785

174

175

174. Two game pie dishes: (left) molded with dead game and vine festoons, with hare finial. Height 7½ ins., width 11½ ins.; (right) ornamented with vine leaves and cauliflower finial. Height 5 ins., width 7 ins. Dishes of this type were introduced c. 1798 during the period of flour shortage to simulate pastry, and production was continued for about 80 years. Both impressed WEDGWOOD.

175. Pair of gilded canopic inkstands with rosso antico reliefs of 'Egyptian hieroglyphs.' Height 5 ins. Impressed WEDGWOOD. c. 1802

176. Vase or flower-holder in the form of four lengths of cut bamboo, painted in blue and standing upon a 'grassy mound' base painted in shades of green. Height 10½ ins. Impressed WEDGWOOD. c. 1785

177. Two wine coolers: (left) White stoneware with green arabesque ornament; (right) cane ware with rosso antico stylized leaf ornament. Both have molded ornament on the lower part and split handles. Height 9½ ins., diameter at lip 6¾ ins. Impressed WEDGWOOD. c. 1820

178. Pair of Cane and white stoneware 'conceits' made during the flour shortage as table centers to simulate confectionery. Length 8 ins. Impressed WEDGWOOD. c. 1800

179. Miniature chamberstick with leaf ornament in gray and lilac, covered with smear glaze. Height 1¾ ins. Impressed WEDGWOOD. c. 1820

180. Engine-turned candlestick in basketwork pattern, on shaped octagonal foot, covered with smearglaze. Height 6¾ ins. Impressed WEDGWOOD. c. 1810

181. Large pot-pourri jar enameled with *feng huang* (Phoenix) and Oriental flowers in the *famille rose* style. These pieces were made with three covers: the first pierced for flowers, the second solid, and the top pierced in a pattern of lozenges and commas. Height 13½ ins. Impressed WEDGWOOD. c. 1820

182. Teapot molded with prunus relief, with 'crabstock' handle and spout, covered with smear-glaze. Impressed WEDGWOOD. c. 1820

183. Antique shape jug with glazed interior, ornamented with gray reliefs of 'Bacchanalian Boys' designed by Lady Diana Beauclerk. Height 5½ ins. Impressed WEDGWOOD. c. 1800

Jasper

The most important of all Wedgwood's inventions, jasper is a fine, dense, white stoneware. Josiah described it as "of exquisite beauty and delicacy, possessing the general properties of the basalt, together with that of receiving colors through its whole surface in a manner which no other body, ancient or modern, has been known to do. This renders it particularly fit for cameos, portraits, and all subjects in bas-relief, as the ground may be made of any color throughout, without paint or enamel, and the raised figures of pure white."

The earlier production of basalt had already provided Josiah with essential experience in the use of turned and applied decoration, and he had assembled a useful collection of models for relief ornament. He was thus able to put into production almost at once a very wide range of ornamental jasper. The body continued for some years to give him trouble, but the introduction of jasper dip (jasper of one color washed or 'dipped' in another) in 1777 helped to solve the problems of the bleeding of color into the white reliefs and the rising cost of cobalt oxide. There were eight basic colors: pale blue, dark blue, green, lilac, yellow, grey, brown and black. Variations on these, giving rise to such descriptions as 'pink,' 'peach' and 'mauve,' were experimental or the accidental results of differing mixtures and firing conditions. Solid jasper (of the same color throughout the body) was withdrawn from general production within a few years of the introduction of jasper dip and was not revived until 1854.

All the earliest jasper objects were on flat backgrounds: seals, cameos, medallions and tablets; but Josiah understood the potential of jasper as a material for the finest vases, and, by patient experiment, succeeded in overcoming the difficulty of fixing large ornament to curved surfaces. The first vases were issued in 1781. Nine years later he was able to show the first of his replicas of the Portland vase (Plate 237). The most beautiful of Wedgwood's original vases was modeled by Flaxman in 1784. Known as the 'Homeric' or 'Pegasus' vase, it is ornamented with reliefs, modeled by Flaxman in 1778 and first used for a large tablet, inspired by the decoration on a Greek calyx-krater from the collection of Sir William Hamilton. Of this tablet, Sir William wrote in July 1786: "I never saw a basrelief executed in the true simple antique style half so well." (Plate 232). The vase, the cover of which is surmounted by a finely modeled figure of Pegasus, was, according to Josiah, "the finest and most perfect I have ever made." He presented a blue and white jasper copy of it to the British Museum (Plate 235).

Among the most interesting of all Wedgwood's great range of jasper wares were the portrait medallions, and of these the most significant are the series of portraits of 'Illustrious Moderns,' which numbered 233 by 1788. Many more were added in Josiah's lifetime, and they have been produced in small quantities since. They remain the largest, the most complete, and the most uniquely fascinating collection of historical portraits ever attempted by a single manufacturer.

Apart from the period 1940-46, jasper has been made continuously from 1775 to the present day, and the greater part has continued to be in the neo-classical style. During the first quarter of the 19th century, Wedgwood produced a similar, but coarser, white stoneware decorated with reliefs in contrasting colors and often covered with smear-glaze. This is often mistaken for jasper, and the body was developed by Josiah I before jasper was perfected in 1775. It is illustrated in this book (Plates 249-251) with jasper for direct comparison.

During the 1850's some pleasing fern and leaf ornaments were created, and towards the end of the century some elongated floral reliefs, tentatively *art nouveau,* made a brief appearance. An ugly purplish-blue dip unfortunately supplanted the original dark blue, and this was used particularly for bas-relief ware produced by covering white stoneware with jasper dip. A lifeless olive-green dip, which bled copiously, made a mercifully brief appearance between 1910 and 1928. From 1929 to 1933 a handsome yellow-buff was made with black reliefs. Crimson dip (Plate 257), introduced in 1925, lasted only seven years owing to severe difficulties with bleeding which could not be overcome. The color was excellent and, when bleeding did not occur, the quality was high. Examples are now much sought-after by collectors. More recent additions have been Royal blue (1953, to commemorate the Coronation of Queen Elizabeth II), Portland blue (1972), Terracotta, with black or white reliefs (1957-59), Lilac (solid, 1960-62), and Primrose (from 1976).

Jasper has been imitated, generally with strikingly inferior results, by manufacturers in Britain, France, Germany, Italy, Russia and Japan. Only the 18th century jasper of Adams and Turner bears comparison with Wedgwood's, and it is easily distinguished from it.

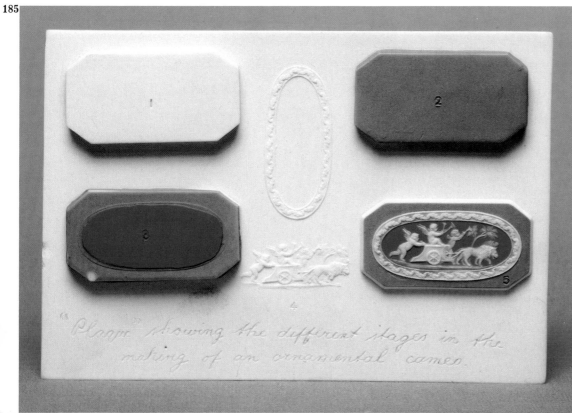

184. A tray of early jasper trial pieces, each marked with a coded description of materials and firing method, and a page from Josiah Wedgwood's Experiment Book. c. 1772-76

185. Jasper plaque, 8¼ ins. by 5½ ins., showing the different stages in the making of a three-color jasper cameo. Impressed WEDGWOOD and O (made by Bert Bentley, c. 1922)

186. Portrait medallion of Benjamin Franklin, white jasper on a blue ground washed (dipped) in yellow-buff. Modeled c. 1777 by William Hackwood after Isaac Gosset. Oval 3¼ ins. by 2¾ ins. Impressed WEDGWOOD & BENTLEY, and FRANKLIN below truncation. c. 1777

187. Blue and white jasper dip portrait medallion of the Marquis de Lafayette (1757-1834), who served under Washington and helped to bring about the defeat of the British army at Yorktown. He was celebrated as 'The Hero of Two Worlds' for his work for the American and French Revolutions. Oval 2 ins. by 1¼ ins. Impressed WEDGWOOD. c. 1790

188. Portrait medallion of Jean-Francois Marie Arouet de Voltaire (1694-1778), friend of Franklin and Jefferson, and a leading European supporter of the American Enlightenment. White jasper portrait on a blue ground dipped in yellow-buff. Oval 3¼ ins. by 2¾ ins. Impressed WEDGWOOD & BENTLEY, and VOLTAIRE below truncation. Modeled by William Hackwood, 1778

189. Blue jasper dip portrait medallion of Edward Bourne with black jasper frame. Bourne was a bricklayer at Etruria, and of this portrait, modeled by Hackwood in 1778, Josiah Wedgwood wrote: "Old Bourne's is the man himself with every wrinkle, crink and cranny in the whole visage." Oval 6½ ins. by 5½ ins. Unmarked, but impressed EDW. BOURNE under the truncation and, surprisingly (for Josiah did not approve of his artists signing their work), signed on the truncation 'Wm. Hackwood 1779.'

190. Very rare solid yellow jasper portrait medallion of George Washington adapted from a medal designed by Voltaire, 1778. Oval 3½ ins. by 2¾ ins. Impressed Wedgwood & Bentley. c. 1778. Wedgwood considered Washington "more absolute than any Despot in Europe," and asked "how then can he be celebrated . . . as the Patron of Liberty?" But he overcame his doubts

191. Exceptionally fine portrait medallion of Josiah Wedgwood, framed in rosso antico and black basalt. Oval 5¼ ins. by 4½ ins. Unmarked. This portrait was modeled by Hackwood in 1782

192. Blue and white jasper plaque, 10 ins. by 13 ins., 'The Judgement of Hercules,' in fine ormolu frame with ribbon tie loop. Modeled by William Hackwood. The figure of Hercules is 7 ins. high, and the relief at the shoulder is ½ in. deep. Impressed WEDGWOOD & BENTLEY. c. 1777

193. Solid blue jasper medallion of Erato, Muse of erotic poetry. Oval 6¼ ins. by 4¾ ins. Impressed WEDGWOOD & BENTLEY. c. 1778

194

195

194. Very large tablet of gray-blue jasper dipped in pale blue of Bacchanalian boys under arbors of panther skins. Modeled after a design by Lady Diana Beauclerk (1724-1808). 22½ ins. by 6 ins. Impressed WEDGWOOD. c. 1787

195. Green dip jasper plaque of 'The Birth of Bacchus,' modeled by Hackwood in 1776. 10½ ins. by 4¾ ins. Unmarked. c. 1778

196. Oval medallion, pale gray-blue jasper with blue dip, height 7 ins. The subject is 'Ganymede and the Eagle.' Impressed WEDGWOOD & BENTLEY. c. 1778

197. Girandole, or wall sconce. Pale blue jasper with white bas-relief of a Herculaneum figure, a female dancer playing cymbals, mounted in a beaded metal frame, with matching jasper candle holders and drip trays set in shaped metal arms. 15 ins. by 8 ins. Marks not visible. c. 1785

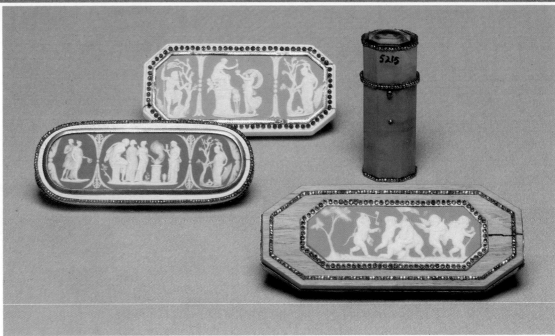

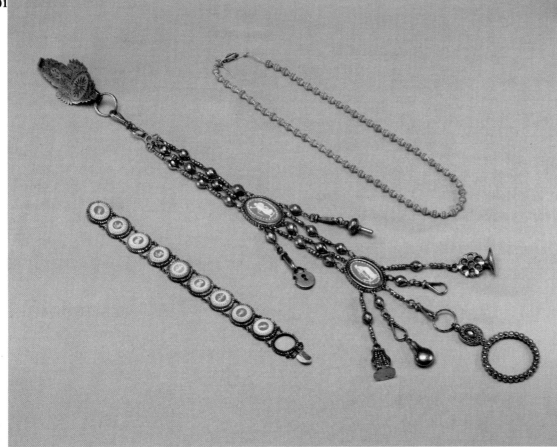

198. Frame of three-color and blue and white jasper cameos, including (center) *Sacrifice to Pomona,* a portrait of George III (center, top) and a cameo celebrating the Anglo-French Commercial Treaty of 1786 (top left). *Sacrifice to Pomona* oval 2¾ ins. by 4 ins.; smallest cameo ½ in. diameter. Various dates c. 1780-90

199. Selection of pin and patch boxes of wood and ivory with gold and cut steel mounts and blue or lilac cameos mounted in the lids. No marks visible. Length 3½ ins. to 4¼ ins. c. 1790

200. Clock pendulum of cut steel mounted with a jasper cameo ornamented with signs of the zodiac, c. 1800; cut steel comb mounted with two jasper buttons and a cameo, c. 1785; and cut-steel mounted cameos of the 'Bourbonnais Shepherd' and 'Poor Maria,' both modeled after designs by Lady Templetown. Heights 2¾ ins. and 3½ ins. Both impressed WEDGWOOD. c. 1785

201. Cut steel chatelaine, or fob chain, mounted with two double-sided jasper cameos with bas-reliefs of 'Fortune' and 'Hope,' and fitted with an eye glass, miniature padlock and key and several seals, length 17 ins.; three-color jasper cameos set in a cut steel bracelet; and a blue and white jasper bead necklace, length 19½ ins. No marks visible. All c. 1785

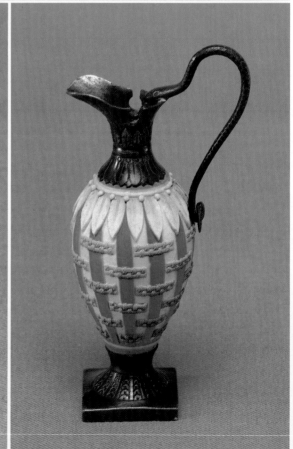

202. Three jasper scent bottles, one ornamented with a portrait of Queen Charlotte, and a cut glass, gold-mounted scent bottle with mounted black and white jasper cameo. No marks visible. All c. 1785-90

203. Two oviform jasper bell pulls: (left) white jasper dipped blue and dipped again in white, engine turned and incised to produce a blue intaglio pattern; (right) white jasper, green dip, with white acanthus and lotus leaf ornament. Height 2¾ ins. No marks visible. c. 1785

204. Sheffield plate mounted miniature jug of blue jasper dip with yellow and white applied ornament, height 4¼ ins. The body is formed from a bell pull (see plate 203), a shape also used for scent bottles. No marks visible. c. 1795

205. Ribbed ivory tortoiseshell, and gold-mounted tea caddy of octagonal shape, each facet being ornamented with a blue and white jasper cameo mounted in gold. Height 5¾ ins. c. 1800

206. Monocular opera glass, the telescopic single lens mounted in ivory and brass, set in a tube of blue jasper dip ornamented with *Sacrifice to Hymen,* modeled by Hackwood in 1776. No marks visible. Height 3 ins. c. 1787

207

208

198

207. Three jasper can-shape cups and saucers; (left to right) green dip with acanthuis leaf ornament (impressed Wedgwood. c. 1790; blue dip, ornamented with four bas-relief groups in separated compartments. Impressed Wedgwood A. c. 1820. All about 2¾ ins. high, and all with lapidary polished interiors.

208. Three jasper can-shape cups and saucers: (left to right) black dip, diced on the engine-turning wheel, with applied green quatrefoils and white laurel stripes. Impressed WEDGWOOD. c. 1790; white jasper with applied green vine, lilac pendants and grapes, and blue cameos. Impressed WEDGWOOD. c. 1790; green dip with four decorative bands of applied blue squares and green quatrefoils, and three bas-relief groups in separated compartments. Impressed WEDGWOOD. c. 1790. All about 2¾ ins. high, and all with lapidary polished interiors

209. Covered chocolate cup and saucer of solid blue jasper with white relief ornament of floral swags and inverted grasses. Height 5¾ ins. The saucer is of the *trembleuse* type (cf. plate 212), and chocolate cups and saucers are often described as *Trembleuses'*. Impressed WEDGWOOD 5 S. c. 1785

211

12

210. Lilac dip coffeepot, height 8¼ ins., engine-turned, with applied bas-relief ornament *'Domestic Employment'* designed by Lady Templetown, shell terminal to top of handle and leafage terminal to handle base. Impressed WEDGWOOD c. 1783. (Compare blue dip version of the same model, page 180)

211. Lilac dip engine-turned and ornamented teapot, sugar box, tea bowl and saucer, and helmet-shape cream jug. Teapot height 3½ ins. All impressed WEDGWOOD. c. 1785

212. Lilac dip on gray jasper soup cup and saucer *(Ecuelle)*, engine-turned and ornamented. Height 3¾ ins. The saucer is of the *trembleuse* type, with a deep well in the center to accommodate the foot of the cup and help to prevent spillage when held in a trembling hand. Impressed WEDGWOOD 3. c. 1785. The figure '3' appears on some of the finest jasper of this period

213. Helmet jug of solid blue jasper with applied ornament of grasses, floral swags, and anthemion (on foot), and bas-relief 'Maternal Affection' designed by Lady Templetown. Split handle with shell terminal. Height 7¾ ins. Impressed WEDGWOOD. c. 1785

214. Set of eight egg-cups and footed stand, solid blue jasper with simple leaf ornament and scroll border. Cup height 2¼ ins., tray diameter 8¼ ins. The cups have lapidary polished interiors indicating that they may have been intended for use. Impressed WEDGWOOD. c. 1785

215. Green dip teapot, height 4 ins., with bas-relief ornament and leaf borders. Impressed WEDGWOOD. c. 1790

216

217

204

216. Chess set of lilac dip and blue dip standing on a contemporary chess board. The set was designed by John Flaxman RA in 1785, and 130 sets were sold during the following ten years. Height of Queen 3½ ins. All impressed WEDGWOOD. c. 1790

217. Pair of Sphinxes, couchant with wings raised, white jasper on black dip bases with applied ornament. Length 6½ ins. Impressed WEDGWOOD. c. 1785

218. Teapot, 'Empire' shape. Solid gray-blue jasper with applied ornament, 'Charlotte at the tomb of Werther' and 'Sportive Love,' designed by Lady Templetown and modeled by William Hackwood in 1785. Engine-turned foot and lid. The fluted spout and handle terminate in acanthus leaf moldings. Height 6 ins. Impressed Wedgwood. c. 1790

219

220

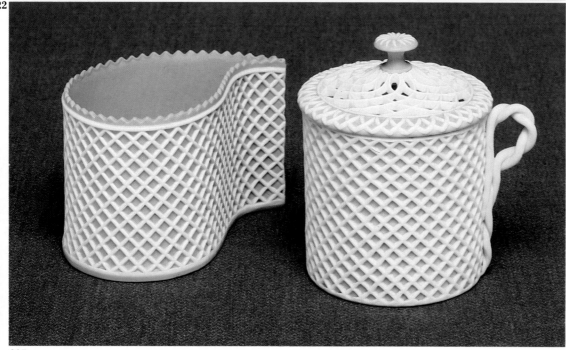

219. *Cabaret (solitaire* with one cup and saucer, *a deux* with two), or Early Morning Tea set, probably the largest group of jasper teaware made during the 18th century. The interiors and rims of the cups were often lapidary polished. Tray 13¾ ins. by 11 ins. All impressed WEDGWOOD except the creamer which is impressed Wedgwood. c. 1784

220. Solid blue jasper bowl on foot with bas-relief ornament of Bacchanalian boys and vine festoons designed by Lady Diana Beauclerk. Lapidary polished interior. Height 5 ins., diameter 9 ins. Impressed WEDGWOOD. c. 1785

221. Solid blue jasper centerpiece bowl with applied white and yellow strapwork in basket weave pattern and applied flowers inside the bowl. Height 9 ins., oval width 9¼ ins. Impressed Wedgwood. c. 1790

222. Two custard cups, one with pierced lid, ornamented with applied latticework. Heights 2 ins. and 2½ ins. Impressed WEDGWOOD. c. 1785

223. Solid blue jasper paint box with white jasper palette and small interior containers for pigments. Wedgwood described his paint chests in the 1779 catalogue: "The paint-chest contains sets of large and small vessels and neat palats [sic] for the use of those who paint in water-colour." Impressed WEDGWOOD. c. 1785

224. Exceptionally fine and large teapot of solid blue jasper with cupid finial, split handle, overlapping leaf spout, and bas-relief ornament designed by Lady Templetown on a 'dimpled' or 'granulated' ground. Sentimental domestic scenes were a popular expression of the Romantic Movement during the last quarter of the 18th century. Height 8 ins. Impressed WEDGWOOD. 1790

225. Ruined column inkstand and taper set, height 4 ins., of solid blue jasper with applied acanthus leaf ornament. Classical ruins and obelisks were fashionable subjects of decoration from about 1750, a vogue inspired by contemporary interest in the excavations of Herculaneum and Pompeii and other classical sites. Wedgwood made a number of these somewhat bizarre objects in jasper as flower holders and ink wells. Impressed WEDGWOOD. c. 1785

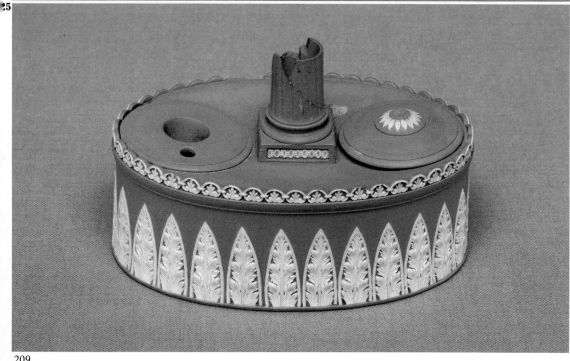

226. Ruined column vase with solid blue jasper base and white broken pillar. Flower holders of this form were made with two or three columns, and also in the shape of broken classical vases. Height 7¾ ins. Impressed WEDGWOOD. c. 1790. See also plate 225

227. Solid blue jasper *seau*, or wine cooler (also used as jardinière) with bas-relief ornament of Bacchanalian boys designed by Lady Diana Beauclerk. Lapidary polished interior. Height 6¼ ins., diameter 7½ ins. Impressed WEDGWOOD. c. 1785

228. Rare violet-blue jasper dip pastille burner with finely pierced lid. Height 5¼ ins. Impressed WEDGWOOD. c. 1785. Pastille burners were used for burning *cassolette* perfumes which helped to disguise the odors of stuffy rooms and their inadequately washed occupants

229

230

212

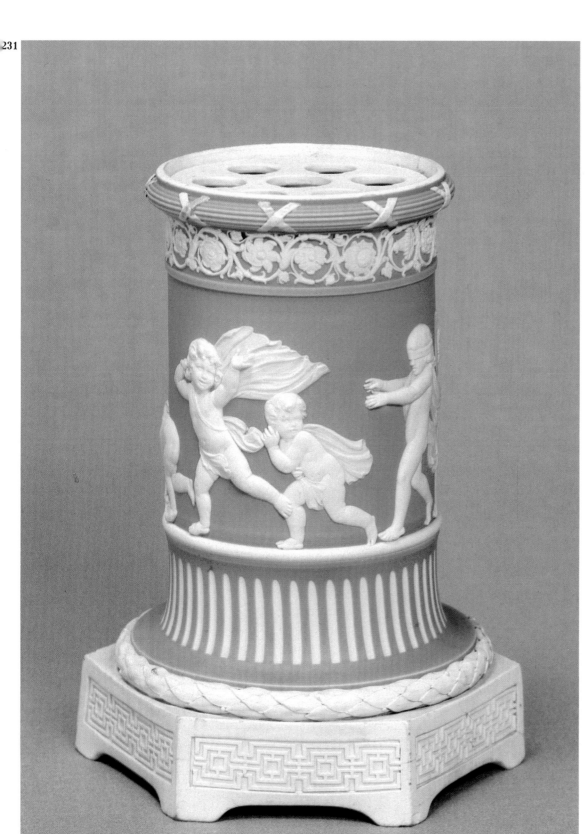

229. Two bulb pots, green dip and solid blue, of square pedestal form with lid for a single bulb. This shape was also used with a perforated lid as a flower holder, and, without lid, as a pedestal for a vase. Designed and modeled by Hackwood. Height 7 ins. Impressed WEDGWOOD. 1796

230. Pair of blue dip pastille or incense burners on dolphin tripod supports, with finely pierced lids. Height 5¼ ins. Impressed WEDGWOOD. c. 1800

231. Cylindrical pedestal bough pot of green jasper dip on solid white jasper hexagonal base. Height 7½ ins. Bas-relief ornament of 'Blind Man's Buff' by Flaxman. This shape was used also for pedestals and lamp bases. Impressed WEDGWOOD. c. 1790

232

233

232. Tablet, 11¾ ins. by 18½ ins., ornamented with 'The Apotheosis of Homer' bas-relief modeled by John Flaxman RA 1777-79. This is probably Wedgwood's most famous bas-relief ornament and was later adapted to ornament a superb vase (plate 235). A companion relief, 'The Apotheosis of Virgil,' was modeled by Flaxman c. 1786. Impressed WEDGWOOD & BENTLEY. c. 1779

233. *Garniture de cheminee* of three blue dip vases, engine-turned, with applied green quatrefoils and blue rectangles in a diced pattern. *Garnitures,* intended for the decoration of chimney pieces, were generally made in sets of three or five. Heights 4¾ ins. and 3¾ ins. Impressed Wedgwood. c. 1790

234. Pale blue-gray jasper vase with snake handles and bas-relief ornament of 'Venus in her Chariot drawn by Swans,' adapted from the work of Charles Le Brun. Height 16½ ins. Impressed WEDGWOOD. c. 1785

235. Greenish-buff dip jasper vase
with Pegasus finial and bas-relief
ornament of 'The Apotheosis of
Homer.' Height 18 ins. This appears
to be a unique example of the
'Homeric Vase,' though fine examples exist in blue dip and black
basalt. Modeled by John Flaxman c.
1786. Impressed WEDGWOOD. c. 1790

236. Pair of miniature solid blue
jasper vases, 6¾ ins. high, with
fluted necks, bas-relief ornament,
and applied anthemion border to
the plinths. Impressed WEDGWOOD.
c. 1785

237. The Portland Vase; (left) blue-black jasper from the original edition of 1790; (right) Portland blue jasper from a limited edition of 1973. Height 10 ins. Vases from the original edition are unmarked except for a number in manganese pencil inside the lip; later versions are impressed WEDGWOOD on the foot-rim or the foot. The copies finished by John Northwood for Wedgwood in 1877 bear the cipher JN above the factory impress mark

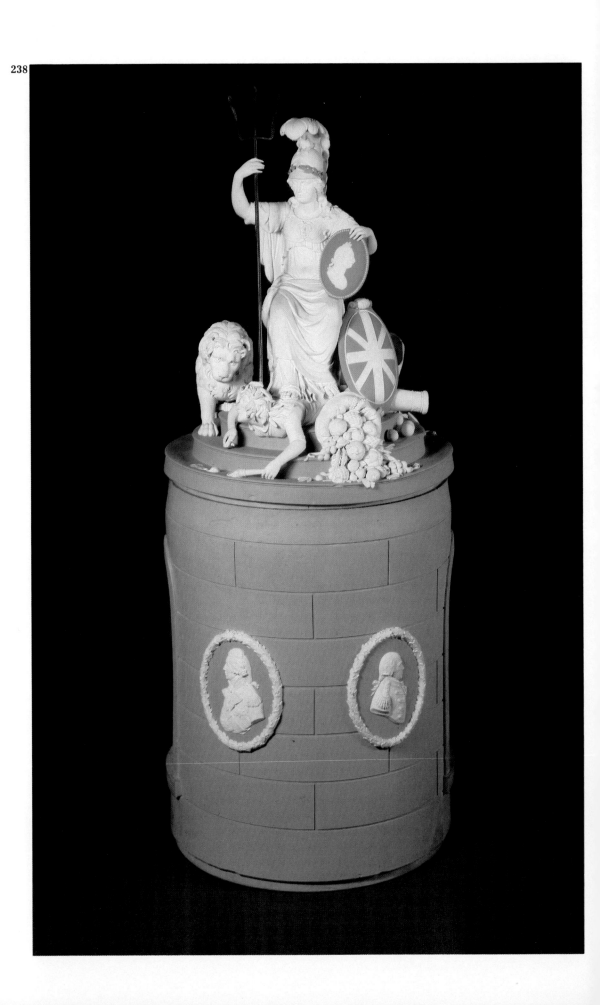

238. 'Britannia Triumphant.' One of Wedgwood's most important jasper groups, modeled by Henry Webber to celebrate British naval victories in the war with France. The tall plinth is ornamented with portrait medallions of Admirals Duncan, Howe, Nelson and St. Vincent, modeled by John De Vaere in 1798. The group, which appears to be the only surviving example, is in a private collection. The plinth is one of two in the Wedgwood Museum at Barlaston. Height, with plinth, 32 ins. c. 1800

239. Pair of solid blue jasper tripod vase-candlesticks with applied white ornament and lions' heads, height 10 ins. (11 ins. with candlestick). The lids are reversible to provide holders for candles. (Cf. Black basalt plate 153). Impressed WEDGWOOD. c. 1810

240

241

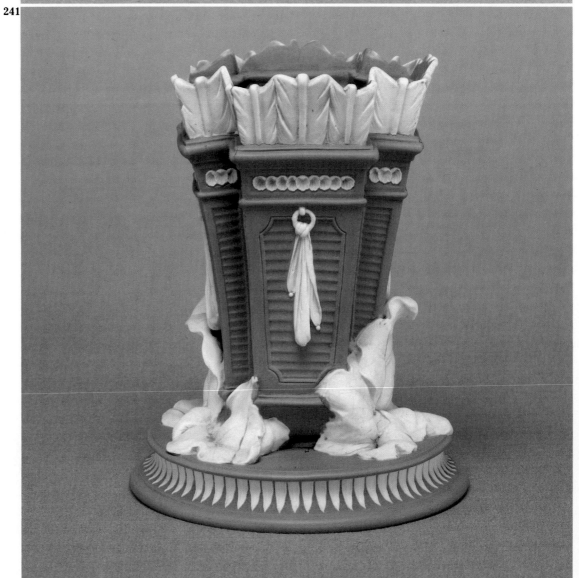

240. Pair of rare yellow dip jasper spill vases with bright blue ornament, height 3½ ins. Impressed WEDGWOOD. c. 1810

241. Vase, height 7 ins., in the form of a quiver molded with panels of horizontal fluting, the arrow flights projecting above the rim. The Quiver Vase was later reproduced in Majolica and bone china. Impressed WEDGWOOD. c. 1800

242. Extremely rare solid white jasper figure of Mercury on a circular blue plinth. Height 9½ ins. overall. Both figure and plinth are impressed WEDGWOOD. c. 1785. All 18th century jasper figures are rare.

243. Pair of rare solid blue and white jasper candlesticks in the form of figures of the goddesses Ceres (left) and Cybele (right). These figures are attributed to Flaxman, c. 1785. Impressed WEDGWOOD. Height 11½ ins.

244. Two chambersticks: (left) green dip with white leaf ornament, extinguisher, and loop for extinguisher. Height 3½ ins. Impressed WEDGWOOD. c. 1810; (right) blue dip, fluted, with leaf ornament. Height 2¼ ins. Impressed WEDGWOOD. c. 1810

245. Pair of solid blue jasper candlesticks, 'Autumn' and 'Winter,' in the form of tree trunks entwined with leaves, with figures of Cupids, one with a basket of grapes, the other with a fire of wood and leaves, emblematic of the seasons. Modeled by William Hackwood. Height 10¾ ins. Impressed WEDGWOOD. c. 1785

246. Pair of solid blue and white jasper candlesticks in the form of Tritons grasping whorled shells (sometimes erroneously described as cornucopia). Catalogued by Wedgwood as 'after Michaelangelo,' these figures, often attributed to Flaxman, may have been the work of William Keeling. Height 11 ins. Impressed WEDGWOOD. c. 1785. These candlesticks, which also appear in black basalt, have been frequently reproduced by Wedgwood

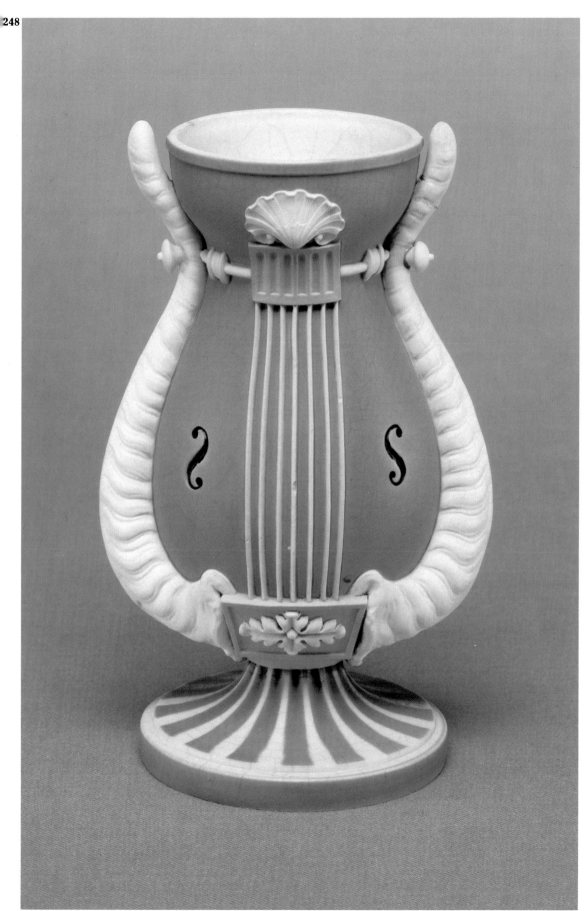

247. Pair of candelabra of cut glass with black and white jasper drums mounted in ormolu. The drops are of yellow and white glass. No marks visible. c. 1790

248. Viol da Gamba vase of blue jasper dip 'to be used either as a flower pot, bulbous-root, or candlestick.' Height 6½ ins. Unmarked. c. 1801

250

251

249. White stoneware bough pot and pot-pourri vase (lacking pierced lid) ornamented with chocolate jasper vine border and smear-glazed. This dual-purpose shape was also made in black basalt, sometimes painted in encaustic colors, in the 18th century. Impressed WEDGWOOD. c. 1810-20. Height 7 ins., diameter 13 ins.

250. White stoneware vase decorated with lilac jasper dip and bright blue jasper acanthus leaf ornament. Height 3¼ ins. Impressed WEDGWOOD. c. 1810-20

251. White stoneware vases (lacking pierced grids), also used as small pedestals, ornamented with bright blue jasper bas-reliefs. The interiors are smear-glazed. Height 4¾ ins. Impressed WEDGWOOD. c. 1810-20

252. Pair of jasper dip wine coolers ornamented with water lily relief decoration. Height 11½ ins. Impressed WEDGWOOD. c. 1850. These wine coolers provide an interesting example of Wedgwood's efforts during the 19th century to find suitable relief ornament that was not of classical origin

253. Black and white jasper vase, height 21¼ ins., ornamented with leaf borders, satyr's head handles and bas-relief of 'The Dancing Hours' modeled by John Flaxman RA c. 1777. The design is adapted from a Greek relief of the 1st or 2nd century BC formerly in the Villa Borghese and now in the Louvre. The figures were remodeled by Hackwood in 1802. They appear on vases, teapots, kettles, tablets and small objects such as salt cellars. This vase, produced in 1905, provides a fine example of Wedgwood's almost continuous reproduction of 18th century models. Impressed WEDGWOOD

254. Remarkable jasper *Plateau*, height 15¼ ins., width 21½ ins., reputedly owned by President Harding and given by him to his secretary. Impressed WEDGWOOD on base of candlestick only. c. 1900

255. Turquoise dip jasper teapot, 146 shape. This rare color was produced for a short period, c. 1875-85, but the quality does not compare favorably with jasper of the 18th century. Impressed WEDGWOOD. c. 1880

256. Three-color jasper dip Trophy plate, diameter 8¾ ins. The center ornament of 'Aurora' was modeled by Hackwood in 1773. Approximately 170 reliefs are used to ornament Trophy plates. Impressed WEDGWOOD MADE IN ENGLAND with special gold backstamp describing the Museum Series of 1978. Trophy plates have been made since about 1860

257. Crimson jasper dip teapot and spill vase, the latter with acanthus and tall lily bas-relief ornament. Crimson jasper was produced only between 1925 and 1932, though experimental quantities had been made some years earlier, and is consequently rare. It was never available in large quantities owing to the tendency of the color to 'bleed' in firing and stain the white relief ornament. Teapot impressed WEDGWOOD ENGLAND. c. 1928; spill vase impressed WEDGWOOD MADE IN ENGLAND and elongated O. Height 7½ ins. c. 1930

258. Spill vase, height 2½ ins. of twice-dipped jasper — dark blue over crimson over white — with sgraffito and trailed slip ornament. The inscription 'H.B. trial 5.2.98' is applied in pale blue. Pale blue and white jasper mug, height 6 ins., with applied floral decoration. Both are the work of Harry Barnard, potter, Museum Curator, and author of Chats of Wedgwood Ware. Spill 1898, mug c. 1902

259. Blue and white jasper medallion, 4¾ ins. diameter, 'Sun and Wind,' designed by Anna Zinkeisen (1901-78) in 1924. Impressed WEDGWOOD (sans serif) MADE IN ENGLAND 57. 1957

260. Portrait medallion of H.M. Queen Elizabeth II produced to celebrate the Queen's Silver Wedding. Modeled by Arnold Machin RA, 1971. Oval 4½ ins. by 3¼ ins. Impressed WEDGWOOD (sans serif) MADE IN ENGLAND 72

261

262

238

261. Wedgwood's first jasper Christmas Plate, 1969 and the first Christmas mug, 1971. 8 ins. diameter; mug height 4½ ins. These commemorative pieces have become extremely popular, and the first editions are already keenly sought by collectors

262. 'Paul Revere's Ride,' one of the plates from the series of six issued to commemorate the bicentennial of American Independence. 1976. Impressed WEDGWOOD (sans serif) MADE IN ENGLAND

263. Tenth Anniversary Christmas Plate ornamented with bas-reliefs from all the previous years' plates. Diameter 9½ ins. Impressed WEDGWOOD (sans serif) MADE IN ENGLAND with commemorative backstamp printed in gold. 1979

264. The American Bicentennial Goblet, of three-color jasper dip ornamented with portrait medallions of Washington and Jefferson. Impressed WEDGWOOD (sans serif) MADE IN ENGLAND 75 and printed with descriptive backstamp in gold. Height 4¾ ins.

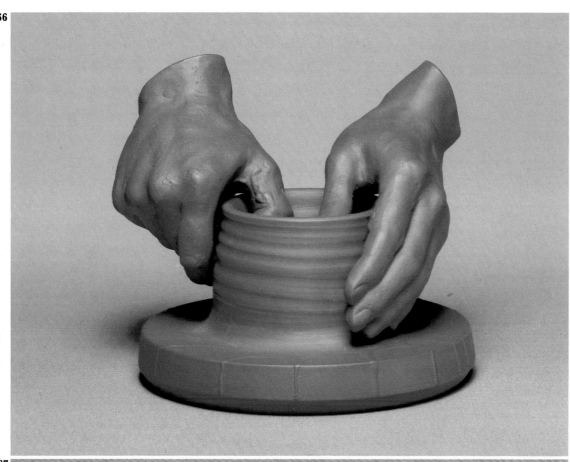

265. Primrose jasper Trophy plate ornamented with terracotta jasper, diameter 9 ins. One of the pieces made for the 'Egyptian Collection' of limited editions, 1978. Impressed WEDGWOOD (sans serif) MADE IN ENGLAND

266. 'The Hands of the Potter,' sculpture by Colin Melbourne of terracotta jasper, issued in a limited edition in 1978. Height 7 ins. Impressed WEDGWOOD (sans serif) MADE IN ENGLAND 78

267. Three-color jasper jewelry, gold-mounted, from a collection of cameos mounted in rhodium plated silver, gold-plated silver, and gold. 1979

Rosso Antico

Red stoneware, in imitation of the Chinese wares of Yi-hsing first exported to Europe in the 17th century, had been common in Staffordshire for 70 years by the time Josiah Wedgwood made his first red ware, decorated with sprigged ornament or engine-turned patterns, in 1764. He thought little of it. To Bentley's suggestion that it might be more widely used, he replied coolly in September 1776: "My objection to it is the extreme vulgarity of red wares. If it had never been made in T. pots and the commonest wares my objections would not have existed." Evidently Bentley pressed his case, for three months later Wedgwood wrote to him: "I will try to imitate the Antico Rosso from your description, but when I have done my best I am afraid where one spectator thinks of Antico Rosso a hundred will be put in mind of a Red teapot."

The rosso antico produced from 1776 was a stoneware which varied in color from brick-red to chocolate, and it subsequently appeared with applied ornament in black or white (Plates 268, 271), with engine-turned decoration (Plate 269), and as sprigged ornament for black basalt (Plate 160), or, more rarely, cane (Plate 175). Much of the rosso antico with black reliefs in the Egyptian style (Plate 275) belongs to the early years of the 19th century, inspired by Napoleon's Egyptian campaign of 1798 and Nelson's victory at Aboukir Bay. To this period also belongs the ornament in the form of so-called hieroglyphs. From 1810, rosso antico was enameled in the *famille rose* style.

Like other stonewares, rosso antico requires no glaze, but vessels intended for liquids were glazed inside to prevent staining. Later in the 19th century Wedgwood produced a porous terracotta body which was used for teasets and coffeesets with enameled decoration, and for simple jugs and water bottles, some with inlaid lines or checkered designs.

268. Vase ornamented with black basalt bas-relief 'Procession of the Deities.' modeled c. 1788 in Rome after the 'Puteal [well-head] of the Twelve Gods' now in the Capitoline Museum. Height 18 ins. Impressed WEDGWOOD c. 1792.

269

269. Two rare rosso antico vases, dipped in black basalt and engine-turned. The right-hand vase has a glazed interior. Unmarked. Height (left) 6¾ ins. (right) 7 ins. c. 1785

270. Very rare medallion of 'Venus and Cupid,' rosso antico relief on black basalt. Oval height 6¼ ins. Unmarked and possibly a trial piece, c. 1780

271

272

248

271. Inkstand of rosso antico with white reliefs in the Egyptian style. 6 ins. diameter. Impressed WEDGWOOD c. 1785

272. Teapot, parapet shape, with white prunus relief and 'crabstock' handle, spout and finial (Cf. Cane plate   ). Height 4¾ ins. Impressed WEDGWOOD. c. 1810

273. Bough pot with pierced lid, ornamented with prunus relief in white. Impressed WEDGWOOD. Height 5 ins. c. 1815

274. Bough pot and pot-pourri vase, enameled in the *famille rose* style, with three covers: the first pierced for flowers, the second solid, and the third (lid) pierced in a pattern of lozenges and commas. Height 13½ ins. Impressed WEDGWOOD A. c. 1815

275. Teapot in the fashionable Egyptian taste with alligator finial and 'Egyptian' reliefs in black. Height 4 ins. c. 1805

276. Candlestick in the Egyptian taste, with sphinx monopodia and black relief ornament. Height 7 ins. Impressed WEDGWOOD. c. 1800

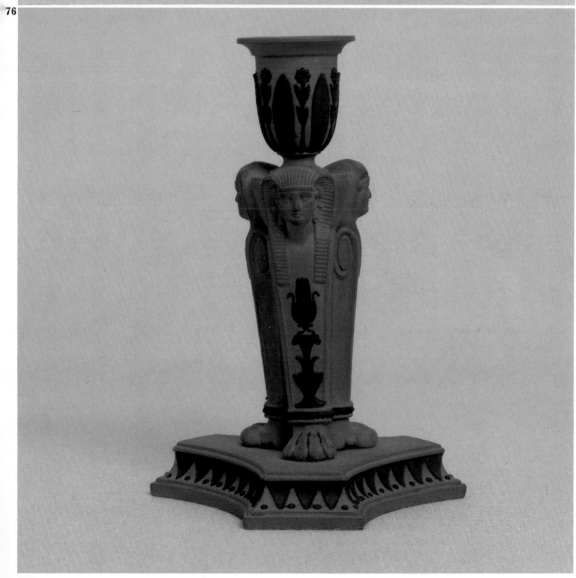

Drab Ware

A form of drab ware, a distinctive greenish-brown stoneware covered with salt-glaze, was produced in Staffordshire in the 1740s. It was generally intended for domestic articles such as teapots and jugs, often with white clay handles and spouts and attractive white slip decoration. Wedgwood's drab ware was introduced in two forms between 1800 and 1820. The earlier, a dry body stoneware, was used mainly for decorative objects. The later version was a stained earthenware, of similar color, primarily for tableware. Drab stoneware was often ornamented in contrasting colors, and drab reliefs were also occassionally used to ornament cane ware. Among the more interesting objects made in the dry body were 'Gothic jugs' (Plate 281). The earliest, catalogued in 1817, appears to have been the forerunner of many such pieces which achieved great popularity in the 1840s, especially from the factories of Charles Meigh & Son, T.J. & J. Mayer, and Ridgeway's. Production of drab stoneware ceased about 1860, but the earthenware of this color has been reintroduced as tableware for Tiffany's, New York, and a mug, designed by Richard Guyatt, was produced to commemorate the Silver Wedding of Queen Elizabeth II in 1973.

277. Silver shape teapot, sugar box and creamer of plain Drab stoneware. Teapot height 4 ins. Impressed WEDGWOOD. c. 1815

278. Oval meat dish, length 16 ins., of drab Queen's ware, printed in black with the arms of the Prince of Denmark and lined in gold. Impressed WEDGWOOD. 1822

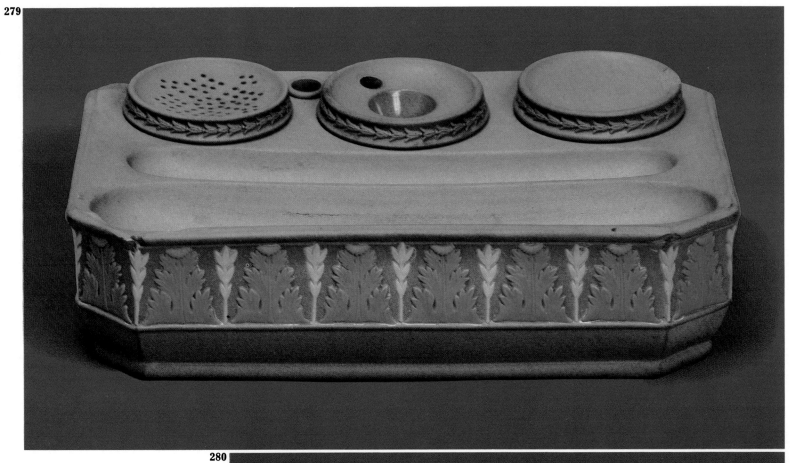

279. Inkstand of Drab stoneware with applied acanthus and laurel ornament in lilac and pale green. 8 ins. by 5½ ins. by 2 ins. Impressed WEDGWOOD. c. 1810

280. Drab Queen's ware teacup and saucer with molded prunus relief, gold line and handle, and robin's-egg blue glazed interior. Impressed WEDGWOOD. Height 3½ ins. c. 1820

281. Drab stoneware Gothic style jug with molded decoration and applied acanthus ornament in pale turquoise. Height 4¾ ins. Impressed WEDGWOOD. c. 1825

282. Smear glazed turned Drab stoneware Dutch jug with white ornament after a design by Lady Templetown. Impressed WEDGWOOD. c. 1825-30

III. Porcelain

Bone China

Bone china, an English invention, was first manufactured at Etruria in 1812 in response to continuous demands for porcelain teasets. Although the use of bone ash in porcelain had been known for many years, the invention of bone china is usually attributed to Josiah Spode II, about 1799, since he appears to have been the first to recognize the value of calcined bone in large proportions. Wedgwood's bone china did not at first succeed, and it was progressively withdrawn from production from 1817, although orders were completed as late as 1829. Bone china of this first period was decorated with painted landscapes by John Cutts (Plate 286), designs of birds and flowers by Aaron Steele and others, and printed or print and enamel patterns in the Oriental styles popular during the Regency period. Wedgwood's designs were, however, too restrained for a public accustomed to associate porcelain with luxury and opulence, and they failed to sell. This unexpected failure provides an instructive example of tradition being allowed to exercise damaging control.

Manufacture of bone china was resumed in 1878 and has continued ever since. The banquet service ordered for the White House in 1910 is some measure of Wedgwood's reputation for quality in bone china tableware early in the century, but it was not until the introduction of the Ordinary Lustres and Fairyland Lustre during the First World War that Wedgwood was able to take the lead among manufacturers of ornamental porcelain. Neglected for some 30 years, Fairyland Lustre has enjoyed an impressive revival in popularity with a consequent rise in sale prices. The richness of the underglaze coloring, combined with lustres and gold printing, and the fantastic and often grotesque figures, scenes and landscapes, have a special appeal which is not to everyone's taste, though the high quality and decorative brilliance are undeniable (Plates 302-305).

Modern Wedgwood bone china, principally tableware, is white and translucent, combining beauty with great strength. It is exported all over the world.

283. Fruit bowl painted with pattern no. 492, Botanical Flowers, gold edge. Printed mark WEDGWOOD in red. Height 6½ ins. c. 1813

284. Parapet teapot with matching sugar box and creamer in pattern 470, 'Gold edge.' Printed mark WEDGWOOD and number 470 in red

285

286

285. Compotier painted with Chinese figures by John Cutts, oval 9 ins. by 5 ins. Cutts (1772-1851) is principally noted for his landscape painting on bone china at the Pinxton and Wedgwood factories. He also painted flowers. For some reason Josiah II had a low opinion of his work, for which he was paid five shillings a day. Printed mark WEDGWOOD in red. c. 1814

286. Teaset painted with landscapes by John Cutts. Each piece is painted with the name of the view on the back. These hand-painted 'named views' are descendants of those first produced in 1773-74 for the 'Frog' service made for Catherine the Great. Teapot height 6 ins. Printed mark WEDGWOOD in red. c. 1814

287. Teaset printed on glaze with *Chinese Tigers* pattern no. 622 in green. The name is confusing since the figures are 'Dogs of Fo' (Lions of Buddha). This pattern was also produced in red, blue and black prints, and the red and green versions are reproduced today. Teapot height 6 ins. All printed mark WEDGWOOD in red. c. 1814

288. Rare bough pot painted with landscapes in purple. Pattern no. 701. Height 3½ ins. Printed mark WEDGWOOD in red. c. 1815

289. Finely painted dessert plates, diameter 8½ ins., decorated with birds by Aaron Steele, who was highly regarded as a painter of 'Etruscan' (encaustic) painted vases at the Chelsea Decorating Studio from 1784. Printed mark WEDGWOOD in red. c. 1815

290. Superb large vase, height 37¼ ins., painted by Thomas Allen (1831-1915). Allen was Art Director at Etruria from 1880 to 1905, and was widely regarded as the finest figure painter of his time. c. 1880

291

292

291. 'Lazy Susan' set, hexagonal shapes with molded fluting and floral pattern printed in olive-green, on matching revolving tray. The coffeepots are fitted with pewter spigots and were probably designed for raised stands which are now missing. Revolving trays of this kind are very rare. Printed mark WEDGWOOD and Portland vase outline in green. c. 1885

292. White bone china shell shapes on stands in the form of branches of coral. Shells, of which Josiah I had a collection, were a typical rococo theme which again became popular toward the end of the 19th century. Heights 7 ins. and 5 ins. Printed mark WEDGWOOD and Portland Vase outline in brown. c. 1790

293. Lidded vase with turquoise enamel groundlay, gold print, and raised gold floral swags. The acorn finial and ram's head handles are typical neo-classical forms, and this shape was first introduced in the 18th century for black basalt. Height 8½ ins. Printed mark WEDGWOOD and Portland Vase outline in blue. c. 1890

294

295

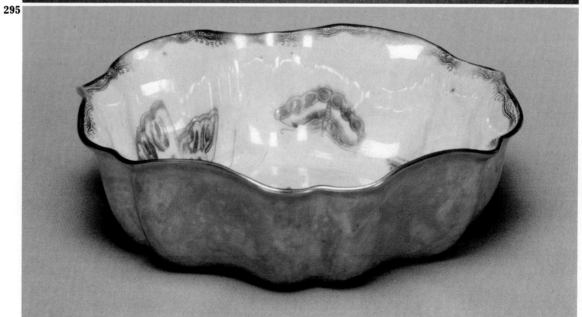

294. Elaborately decorated and gilt plate, diameter 9¼ ins., with pierced border, yellow groundlay, and hand-painted landscape in brown. This type of lavish decoration is typical of late Victorian and Edwardian taste for opulence. Printed mark WEDGWOOD and Portland Vase outline in blue. c. 1900

295. Scalloped bowl, the interior decorated with Butterfly lustre pattern, the exterior with gold-printed butterflies on a mottled orange lustre ground. Diameter 8 ins. Printed WEDGWOOD ENGLAND and Portland Vase outline in gold. c. 1916

296. Powder blue ground and gold printed Dragon lustre hexagonal vase, pattern no. Z4829, the interior with pale green staining and mother-of-pearl lustre. Height 13½ ins. Printed mark WEDGWOOD MADE IN ENGLAND and Portland Vase outline in gold. c. 1914

297

297. Bone china Water Ewer (Cf. black basalt plate 147). Height 14½ ins., decorated in enamel colors and gold. Printed mark WEDGWOOD and Portland Vase outline. c. 1900

298. Bone china 'Michelangelo vase' (Cf. black basalt plate   ), height 13 ins., decorated in enamel colors and gold. Printed mark WEDGWOOD and Portland Vase outline. c. 1900

299. Pair of mottled blue ground and gold printed Dragon lustre vases, height 13¼ ins. Printed mark WEDGWOOD and Portland Vase outline in gold. c. 1915

300. Bud vase, height 5 ins., decorated with mother of pearl lustre and gold-printed butterflies, pattern no. Z4832. Printed mark WEDGWOOD ENGLAND and Portland Vase outline in gold. Pattern no. in gray

301. Coral and bronze 'Willow Fairyland' cigarette box, length 7 ins. Pattern Z5406. Printed mark WEDGWOOD MADE IN ENGLAND and Portland Vase outline in gold. c. 1920

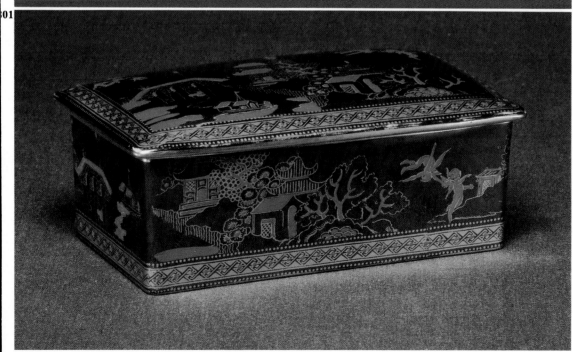

302. Fairyland Lustre octagonal bowl, diameter 7½ ins., decorated with 'Firbolgs' pattern Z5200. Ruby ground overlaid with orange and then ruby lustre. Printed mark WEDGWOOD ENGLAND and Portland Vase outline in gold. c. 1920

303. Fairyland lustre 'Candlemas' vase, height 7 ins., pattern no. Z5157. Printed mark WEDGWOOD ENGLAND and Portland Vase outline in gold. c. 1920

304. Fairyland Lustre plate, diameter 13 ins., decorated with 'Imps on a Bridge and Tree House,' pattern Z4968. The back of the dish is lustred in dark blue and peacock green. Painted mark Z4968 in black. No printed marks. c. 1920

305. Fairyland lustre Persian cup, diameter 10 ins., decorated with 'Leapfrogging Elves.' Printed mark WEDGWOOD ENGLAND and Portland Vase outline in gold. c. 1925

306

307

306. Lidded soup cup and saucer and sugar bowl decorated with black glaze and semi-abstract patterns in platinum by Louise Powell, grand-daughter of Emile Lessore. Printed mark WEDGWOOD MADE IN ENGLAND and Portland Vase outline in brown, with Louise Powell's monogram in platinum and pattern nos. (soup cup & saucer) 3724 and (bowl) 4188. c. 1935

307. 'St. Paul's Cathedral.' One of a series of six designs on bone china plates, diameter 6 ins., by Lawrence Whistler (b. 1912). Celebrated as one of the greatest of modern glass engravers, Whistler designed these 'Outlines of Grandeur,' to represent famous architecture characteristic of six periods of British history, in 1956. Special descriptive backstamp incorporating WEDGWOOD MADE IN ENGLAND. These designs were also produced on Lincoln shape plates, diameter 10¾ ins.

308. Argonaut shell center in Alpine Pink bone china. Height 8½ ins. Printed mark WEDGWOOD Alpine Pink Bone China MADE IN ENGLAND and Portland Vase outline in green. c. 1936

309

310

311

312

309. Pair of plates from the set of six silk-screen designs by the distinguished sculptor Eduardo Paolozzi in 1970 and entitled *Variations on a Geometric Theme*. The plates were produced in a limited edition of 200 sets. Diameter 10½ ins.

310. Plate, diameter 10¾ ins., printed in gold with *Persephone* border designed by Eric Ravilious and the Royal Coat of Arms. This service was made specially for the Foreign Secretary's banquet to celebrate the Coronation of Queen Eliabeth II in 1953. The plates have a gilded foot-rim. Printed mark WEDGWOOD BONE CHINA MADE IN ENGLAND. 1953

311. Windsor Castle. One of a set of six views of British castles designed by David Gentleman in 1977 and issued in a limited edition of 500 sets. Diameter 10½ ins. Descriptive backstamp and Portland Vase outline

312. 'Chou Dynasty' bowl designed by Susie Cooper in 1979, the design taken from a wine bucket, c. 11th century. 9¾ ins. diameter. Susie Cooper (b. 1903) was particularly noted in the 1930s for her designs influenced by art nouveau and art déco styles. Her company, established in 1932, was one of the first acquired by Wedgwood in the formation of the Wedgwood Group of companies

Parian is a white porcelain-like body, slightly translucent, first marketed by Copeland under the name of 'Statuary Porcelain' in 1846, and named by Minton after the fine white marble quarried near the summit of Mount St. Elias on the Greek island of Paros. It was used, generally unglazed, and without color, mainly for busts or figures. Wedgwood's Parian was introduced in 1849 and named after the statuary marble from the quarries at Carrara in Northern Italy. The name did not become widely accepted, and the term 'Parian' is more commonly used to describe similar wares from all factories. Many of Wedgwood's 18th century busts and figures were reproduced in the Carrara body and others, by or after the work of William Beattie (Plate 317), E.W. Wyon and Carrier de Belleuse were modeled specially for the new body. A list of models available in 1859 includes 53 figures, 15 groups and 22 busts, besides candlesticks, spill vases and honey pots, but surprisingly few seem to have survived. Carrara was withdrawn from production in 1880.

Between 1866 and 1880, to compete with the decorative porcelain of Minton and Worcester, Wedgwood produced vases of glazed Parian. These were reproductions of 18th and early 19th century shapes, originally designed for basalt or jasper, and they were heavily ornamented in relief, with enameled grounds and gilding (Plates 318-319). They were evidently not produced in great quantity and examples are comparatively rare. Since Queen's ware vases with similar decoration were made at about the same time, the glazed Parian vases are often mistaken for them. The Parian body, however, is whiter and more obviously vitrified, and the relief ornament, although glazed, is sharper than the Queen's ware reliefs.

313. Carrara bust of Venus, height
15 ins. including socle. Impressed
WEDGWOOD on truncation of
shoulder. c. 1855

314
315

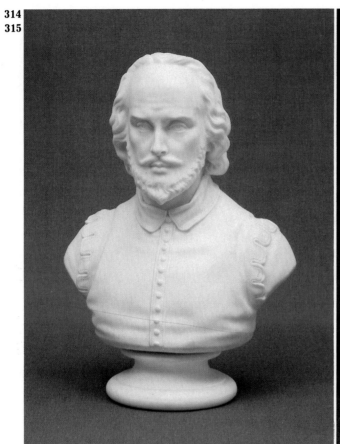

316

314. Bust of Shakespeare by Felix Miller, modeled for the tercentenary of Shakespeare's birth, 1864 (Cf. black basalt plate 135). Height 12 ins. Impressed PUBLISHED UNDER THE SPECIAL PATRONAGE OF THE SHAKESPEARE NATIONAL COMMITTEE BY HOWELL, JAMES & CO, LONDON, APRIL 24th 1864 F.M. MILLER Sc. WEDGWOOD

315. 'Ireland.' One of a set of three figures representing England, Scotland and Ireland, modeled by William Beattie. Height 13 ins. Impressed WEDGWOOD. c. 1858. Beattie, a sculptor and modeler, worked at Etruria from 1856 to 1864. He also modeled figures for the Minton and Copeland factories

316. Bust of George Stephenson (1781-1848. Inventor and founder of railways). Height 14½ ins. Impressed on back of shoulders: G. STEPHENSON JOSIAH WEDGWOOD & SONS PUBLISHED JULY 12 1858 E.W. WYON F

317. 'The Sacrifice' (Abraham sacrificing Isaac), modeled by William Beattie. 24 ins. by 14 ins. Impressed WEDGWOOD. c. 1857

318. Glazed Parian vase with cupid finial, heavily ornamented and gilded on enameled grounds. The shape and relief ornaments are reproduced from 18th century molds intended for jasper and basalt. This, and the more restrained vase in the following illustration, are examples of Wedgwood's efforts to compete with the ornamental porcelain vases of other English manufacturers. Height 12½ ins. Impressed WEDGWOOD. c. 1875

319. Glazed Parian vase with enameled grounds ornamented with signs of the Zodiac. Height 11 ins. Impressed WEDGWOOD. c. 1875

3 How Wedgwood is Made

THE CERAMIC BODIES

All Wedgwood wares may be divided into three main types of ceramic body: earthenware (pottery), stoneware, and porcelain.

Earthenware is opaque and remains porous after the first (biscuit) firing. The main ingredients are calcined flint, ball clay, china clay (kaolin) and china stone (similar to china clay but at an earlier stage of decomposition). Wedgwood's earthenwares include Queen's ware (creamware and colored bodies), Pearl ware and majolica.

Stoneware is a hard, vitreous and generally opaque body mid-way between earthenware and porcelain. The ingredients vary considerably, but clay and fusible rock are common to them all. Wedgwood's stonewares ('dry bodies') include Jasper, Black Basalt, Rosso Antico, Cane, and Drab ware. Stonewares are not porous but may be stained by liquids. They are, therefore, usually glazed if they are intended to be used for food or drink, or as flower holders or vases.

Porcelain is a vitreous semi-translucent body, originally made from white clay, feldspathic stone and silica (e.g. Chinese porcelian – 'true porcelain'). Bone china is an English porcelain of which about fifty per cent is calcined animal bone, the remainder being mainly china stone and china clay. It is noted for its great strength, whiteness and translucency. Carrara (Parian) is a form of porcelain made from china clay, feldspathic rock and frit (a glassy compound of white sand, Cornish stone and potash). It is best known in the white, unglazed (biscuit) form in which it was generally used in the 19th century for busts and figures, but glazed, enameled and gilt vases were also made by Wedgwood in small quantities between 1866 and 1880.

THE FORMS
Clay shapes are formed by two principle methods: throwing and casting.

Throwing is one of the oldest methods of shaping clay vessels and has remained almost unchanged except that the thrower's wheel is now turned by an electric motor. The speed is controlled by a foot pedal, leaving the potter's hands free to work the clay. A weighed ball of carefully prepared soft clay mixture, the ingredients varying according to the ceramic body employed, is thrown onto the center of the wheel. The thrower works the rotating mass up and down until he is satisfied that the clay is of even consistency and is running true on the wheel. He is then ready to open out the clay, pushing his thumb into the center and pulling the pot upwards into a cylindrical shape.

Throwing

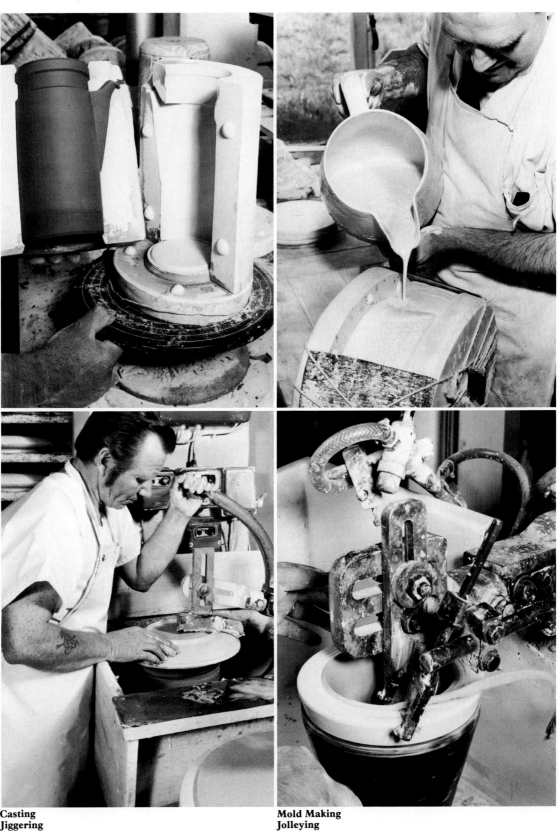

Casting
Jiggering

Mold Making
Jolleying

With one hand inside and the other outside, he presses the shape up and outward until he achieves the form required. The thrown pot is then cut away from the wheel with a short length of wire and set aside to dry until it reaches the state known as cheese-hard or leather-hard. Throwing is, of course, possible only for objects of circular section. It requires a true craftsman's sensitivity and skill. In the cheese-hard state, the shape may be refined by turning (shaving) it on a lathe.

Casting. Pottery which is not of circular section, or which has a molded decoration is most easily made by casting. Slip (liquid clay) is poured into a plaster mold which absorbs much of the water from it. A coating of clay is left on the inside of the mold, the thickness of this coating depending on the length of time the slip remains in the mold. The caster uses his skill and experience to judge when to pour away the surplus slip, leaving the correct thickness of clay adhering to the mold. This contracts as it dries and may be removed when the mold (made in two or more interlocking pieces) is opened. The cast piece is cleaned and all seams left by joins in the mold are smoothed away by hand. Cast handles, spouts and feet are firmly fixed by hand, using a touch of water or slip as adhesive.

Mold Making. Mold making requires skill and precision. From the original model, which may be of clay, wood, wax, plaster or metal, a plaster cast is taken. This is the master reference copy and is known as the *block mold*. From this (intaglio) mold, another solid cast, an exact replica of the original model, is made. This is known as the *case mold*. From case molds, the working (intaglio) molds are made. When the case molds become worn, a fresh one may be made from the block mold. By this method, the original standard of reproduction is maintained for very long periods without the necessity of taking another cast from the model.

Jiggering and Jolleying. Mechanical processes are now used for the making of plates, dishes and cups. Plates and dishes are made upside down by placing a "bat" (pancake) of clay on a revolving disc in the form of a plaster mold, which shapes the inside of the plate, while a profile to form the back is lowered onto it. Surplus clay is removed by hand. This process is known as *jiggering*. Cups are formed in a similar manner on a machine called a *jolley*. A mold forms the exterior of the cup, the profile the interior. Both the jigger and the jolley are developments of the potter's wheel.

ORNAMENT AND DECORATION

Pottery and porcelain may be ornamented by the application of separately molded clay reliefs ('sprigged' ornament), or by cutting designs into the mold in which the piece is to be cast. (integrally cast or molded ornament). Fluted, diced or rouletted patterns may be added by hand or by the use of the engine-turning lathe when the unfired clay is dried to cheese-hardness. Sprigged ornament is used particularly for Wedgwood's jasper and other dry bodies, and for hand-embossed Queen's ware. This technique has remained virtually unchanged for more than 200 years. The figure maker presses clay into pitcher (fired clay) molds reproduced from 18th century originals. Surplus clay is sliced away, and the figure is eased from the mold with a flat spatula and turned out onto a plaster tray. The ornamenter moistens with water the clay surface of the body to be ornamented, and the ornament is laid on and pressed firmly but gently into position. Great care is required to avoid spoiling the details of the ornament, and in the 18th century these details were sharpened by 'undercutting' before the piece was fired. The engine-turning lathe was introduced by Josiah I at the Ivy House Works in 1763 and has been in use ever since. A copy of the original machine, installed at Barlaston in 1976 by Arthur Ward and George Hughes, whose service with Wedgwood totalled 74 years, can operate like the original at speeds between 4 and 555 revolutions per minute.

Ceramic decoration is of many kinds, and all the most important varieties have been employed at some period by Wedgwood. The simplest forms of decoration are those which make use of stained clay, either as a solid body (e.g. Wedgwood's solid blue jasper, *Celadon, Alpine Pink* bone china), or as slip to provide a contrasting pattern or ground color (e.g. jasper dip, some early engine-turned Queen's ware, and pieces designed by Keith Murray in two-color clay). Solid colored clays may also be wedged together to produce veined or marbled effects, and Josiah Wedgwood used this technique as well as the mixing of colors in the glaze to imitate natural stones such as agate and porphyry.

Colored glazes have played an important part in Wedgwood's history, particularly the brilliant Green Glaze still popular today, the glazes used for the decoration of majolica, and the beautiful glazes employed to decorate Norman Wilson Unique ware.

Inlaid patterns are produced by impressing the unfired clay with an intaglio design which is then filled with slip of a contrasting color. Patterns of this kind, in imitation of the so-called *Henri Deux* ware made in the 16th century at Saint-Porchaire in France, were applied to some important ornamental pieces in the 1880s, and simpler decoration of the same type appeared on a range of such household objects as candlesticks, ale jugs and water bottles from 1859.

Engine Turning

Figure Making

**Transfer Printing
Powdering**

**Handpainting
Applying a Transfer**

Hand-painted decoration may be applied under the glaze (when the ware has been fired once and is in the biscuit state) or over the glaze. The palette of underglaze ceramic colors is more limited than that for onglaze decoration, and the most common early colors are cobalt blue and manganese-purple, though many others were added in the 19th century.

Transfer-printing, the process of applying prints taken from engraved copper plates or cylinders to glazed ware, was invented by John Brooks in 1752 and developed independently by John Sadler and Guy Green of Liverpool about 1757. Although Josiah I bought the right to do his own printing in 1763, he continued for many years to send enormous quantities of creamware to Sadler & Green for decorating. A development of this process was print and enamel decoration, ceramic colors being used to fill in printed outlines. Multi-colored transfers (lithographs) offer fine detail and a wider gradation of colors, but their application demands less craftsmanship than print and enamel decoration and they were not used by Wedgwood until 1944.

Rich and interesting effects may be obtained by the use of metal. Gold, applied onglaze and burnished, is now in general use for printed patterns, and most particularly for lines to enrich border patterns on bone china. High quality gold, as used by Wedgwood, is easily recognized by its appearance and strength. Gold of poor quality has a reddish, brassy color and soon shows signs of wear. Although some early pieces, particularly vases, bear traces of gilding, little of Wedgwood's tableware was gilded because gilding of the Wedgwood & Bentley period tended to wear badly and Josiah thought that gold was an unsuitable decoration for earthenware. Bone china has usually been enriched with gold since its introduction in 1812. In modern times platinum has often been used instead of gold.

Gold and other metals may also be employed for the production of lustre wares, and Wedgwood's splashed and mottled lustres, known as 'variegated,' 'marbled' or 'Moonlight' lustre, introduced in 1806, are much sought-after by collectors. A later, and important, development in the use of lustre appears in the Ordinary Lustres and Fairyland Lustre designed between 1915 and 1931. The sponged ('powder') colors used as backgrounds were created in 1912 in imitation of the Chinese *ch'ui ch'ing,* applied by blowing powdered pigment through a bamboo tube, the end of which was covered by a silk screen.

FIRING

Firing. The action of heat on clay, or clay mixed with other materials, is the basis of pottery manufacture. When a piece of clay has been dried and reached a state known as 'white hard,' it is ready to be fired in the biscuit kiln. This first firing takes about 50 hours in modern electric tunnel ovens, and the ware reaches a maximum heat of 1150°c. (porcelain 1240°c.). Underglaze decoration must then be fired on (hardened-on) at 750°c. before glazing. If the piece is not to receive underglaze decoration it is then dipped (glazed) and fired in the glost kiln at a temperature of 1070°c. (porcelain 1120°c.) for about 30 hours. Onglaze patterns must be hardened-on at temperatures between 715°c. and 850°c. to fix them into the glaze (print and enamel decoration requires two separate firings). Gold and platinum require yet another separate firing at 720°-730°c. before it can be burnished. Bone china with print and enamel patterns and gold lines must therefore be fired five times, and some Norman Wilson Unique wares have been fired as many as eight times.

GLAZING

Glazing. Glaze, usually made nowadays from red lead, sand, borax, whiting, Cornish stone and Cornish clay, is a form of glass, applied as a thin, very even covering to biscuit ware. It is used to make earthenware, which is porous in the biscuit state, impermeable, and on vitrified wares (stoneware and porcelain) principally to prevent staining. Glazes also add strength to ceramic bodies and protect decoration. They may be colored (usually by the addition of metallic oxides) or almost colorless, transparent or opaque, glossy or almost matte in appearance. With the exception of ornamental jasper and other dry bodies, and the Carrara body produced in biscuit in the 19th century, all Wedgwood wares are glazed, and some, such as green glazed wares, majolica, and *Moonstone,* rely for their effect largely upon the beauty of the glazes employed.

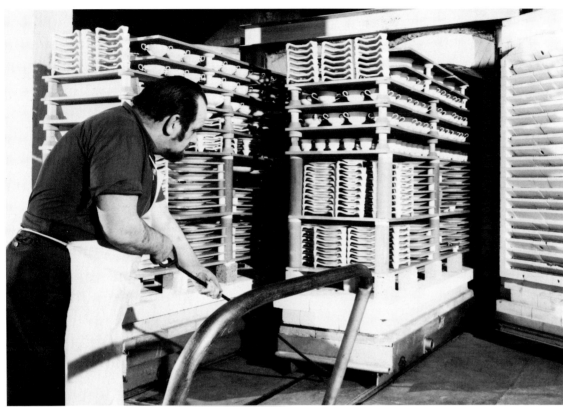

Firing

Glazing

4 Collecting Wedgwood

Collecting is an exercise in taste, knowledge and judgment. The true collector is one whose profit is derived from learning, and the pleasure, aesthetic and intellectual, obtained from the study of his subject. Financial gain is an incidental, but satisfying, tribute to his connoisseurship, but the true collector sells only to improve his collection. The collector is necessarily a specialist, and the narrower the specialization the more he may lay claim to a measure of expertise.

There is no short cut to knowledge of Wedgwood wares. They have been the subject of many books, and the study of scholars and active collectors for at least a century; two museums – the Wedgwood Museum at Barlaston, and the Buten Museum of Wedgwood in Philadelphia – are devoted entirely to them; and yet, so great is the subject, important information and previously unrecorded examples continue to come to light.

Detailed knowledge of his subject is essential to any collector who is not content to depend entirely upon others to form his collection, and this can be acquired only by extensive study. The collector relies primarily on the senses of sight and touch. Museum collections afford the opportunity to see Wedgwood wares of all periods and to compare them with the work of imitators. The larger auction houses and the shops of reputable dealers give the collector the chance to handle the objects, to feel the texture of the ceramic bodies, and to study the marks. No book, however large or authoritative, can be a substitute for this first-hand experience. Scholarly and well-illustrated books are, nevertheless, essential guides, reducing to manageable proportions a study that would otherwise occupy a lifetime, and providing the fundamental structure of knowledge upon which connoisseurship may be built.

Old Wedgwood was being collected in the 19th century, and jasper has always been the ware most sought-after and most highly prized. Eighteenth-century jasper is of particularly fine quality. The surface, smooth not granular, has been compared to that of freshly-cut cheese. The relief ornament is crisp, like carving of the Chippendale period, and the figures and portrait heads show evidence of undercutting that is easily visible under a glass. Undercutting – the technique of sharpening detail with a cutting tool before firing – is most apparent on such features as hair, noses, ears, and the folds of drapery, where they have been cut on a plane parallel with (horizontal to) the plane of the background. Only those details which are at an angle to the background can be reproduced from the mold. Very little jasper was undercut after about 1810, though some good work of this kind was done by Harry Barnard and Bert Bentley in the 1920s.

Early black basalt, too, is specially fine-grained and silken to the touch, with sharp relief ornament. The composition of the body remained unchanged for more than 150 years, and many of the most important models were reproduced until the 1930s, but the ornament of later pieces is less sharply defined. Recognition of period depends on experience and the aid of marks.

Queen's ware of the 18th century, and some belonging to the early years of the 19th century, is surprisingly light in weight. The earliest ware is a deep cream or buff color,

The Wedgwood Collector's Map of Britain

Examples of Wedgwood ware are to be seen in the Art Galleries and Museums of most British cities, and in many of the great houses which are open to the public. This map for collectors shows the largest public collections, houses containing pieces of particular rarity or interest, and a few smaller museum collections chosen for their geographical situation (e.g. in cities of special tourist attraction or in areas where no major public collections exist). The most important specialist collections are shown in capitals.

Glasgow
City Museum &
Art Gallery

Edinburgh
Royal Scottish
Museum

Leeds
City Art Gallery
(Temple Newsam House)

LIVERPOOL
City Museums
Lady Lever Art Gallery
(Port Sunlight)

MANCHESTER
City Art Gallery

STOKE-ON-TRENT
City Museum & Art Gallery
Wedgwood Museum
(Wedgwood factory at
Barlaston)

NOTTINGHAM
City Museum &
Art Gallery (Nottingham Castle)

Norwich
Castle Museum

BIRMINGHAM
Birmingham Museum &
Art Gallery

Northampton
Althorp (Private residence of
Earl Spencer containing
Wedgwood dairy)

Cambridge
Fitzwilliam Museum

Cardiff
National Museum
of Wales

Oxford
Ashmolean Museum

LONDON
British Museum
Victoria & Albert Museum

Salisbury
Salisbury &
South Wiltshire Museum

Hove
Museum of Art

Brighton
Brighton Museum &
Art Gallery

Plymouth
Plymouth Museum
Saltram House
(National Trust)

0   25   50   75   100
MILES

KILOMETERS
0   25   50   75   100

and the glaze, which shows a distinctive green tinge where it has collected under handles or foot-rims, tends to be irregular. After about 1768 the color of the ware is much paler, a creamy-ivory, with paler, evenly-applied glaze. The weight after about 1810 is noticeably greater. Hand-painted decoration is no guarantee of early period since this technique was carried on as late as the 1950s, and hand-enameling over printed outlines has continued to the present day. Sadler & Green printing is quite easily recognized after a few examples have been carefully examined.

Wedgwood wares have been faked since the 19th century, but the quality of the spurious pieces is generally so poor as to deceive no one. Far more deceptive are those genuine Wedgwood pieces, such as vases, which were made in several parts held together by a screw and nut (a method introduced in 1771), and which have been separated from their plinths. It is not difficult to fix a marked Wedgwood & Bentley plinth from a broken basalt vase to a later replica, and it is not unknown for jasper vases, none of which were made during the period of the Wedgwood & Bentley partnership (1769-80), to appear with white jasper plinths which originally belonged to vases of variegated creamware. Marked Wedgwood & Bentley plinths may also be fitted to vases made by other manufacturers, and it is therefore essential to examine every part of a vase with care. With few, very rare, exceptions, Wedgwood vases were marked only on the plinths. If the plinth has been lost or broken, a Wedgwood vase will generally be unmarked.

Before Wedgwood's time, marks on English pottery and porcelain were rarely used, and those which did appear were emblems or devices, pseudo-Chinese ideograms, or names denoting the place of origin. It was Josiah Wedgwood who first properly understood the marketing value of marking wares with the name of the manufacturer. So that it should be permanent and difficult to forge, he had the name impressed in the clay before firing. His mark was used rarely before 1764, more frequently between 1764 and 1768, and generally after 1769. From that date, until Bentley's death in 1780, all ornamental wares were marked WEDGWOOD & BENTLEY (or Wedgwood & Bentley). Useful wares continued to be marked WEDGWOOD (or Wedgwood).

The Wedgwood impressed marks are very difficult to forge. The difference between a mark impressed in the clay before firing and one that has been incised later is immediately obvious even when some attempt has been made to disguise the forgery by varnishing. Forged marks are therefore more likely to appear on faked ware of inferior quality, impressed in the clay at an early stage of production.

Collectors should always examine marks with care. A scratch or elongated dent below the Wedgwood impressed or printed mark is likely to be evidence that the words 'ENGLAND' or 'MADE IN ENGLAND', indicating manufacture after 1891 or 1898, have been ground out. Forms of varnish are often applied to make it appear that the mark left by grinding is under the glaze. Alternatively, the piece may have been glazed again and re-fired, but in such cases heavy crazing usually occurs. The recent rise in the prices of Fairyland Lustre has led to the appearance of lustre pieces, made during the 1920's and 1930's by other factories without any intention to deceive, now bearing spurious printed Wedgwood and Portland vase marks which have replaced genuine marks of other manufacturers removed by grinding. The surface damage done to the base of the object, the poor quality of the spurious marks, and the evidence of varnishing or re-glazing are all easily detectable.

The marks 'VEDGWOOD', 'WEDG WOOD', 'WIEGWOOD', and 'J. WEDGWOOD' all appear in printed or impressed form on wares of other factories, and some good quality creamwares made at the Ferrybridge Pottery, Yorkshire, c. 1790-1800 are impressed 'WEDGWOOD & Co.' Such was Wedgwood's fame on the Continent that porcelain decorated with a blue enamel ground, made at Meissen c. 1785-1815 in imitation of jasper, came to be described as *Wedgwoodarbeit* (literally: Wedgwood work).

Unmarked Wedgwood exists from all periods, but it is safer for a collector without considerable experience to assume that all Wedgwood ware after 1771, at the latest, was marked than to allow himself to be persuaded to buy unmarked pieces as authentic Wedgwood ware. Many of Wedgwood's molds and models were sold in 1828, later to be used by imitators, and many more have been copied by other manufacturers.

Great collections are formed by design. Few collectors can hope to acquire in a single lifetime an important collection comprising fine examples of all types of ware from all periods. The majority will begin with a general collection and subsequently decide to specialize in one body, type of decoration or shape. Even today there is ample opportunity for the collector of modest means to form an interesting collection, particularly of wares of the 19th and 20th centuries. The work of Alfred and Louise Powell, John Skeaping, and Keith Murray, for example, is already collected, and the excellence of Richard Guyatt's designs for commemorative mugs leaves little room for doubt that they will be among the collectors' pieces of the near future.

Fashion plays an important part in determining prices, which may therefore rise or fall. In 1781, when the stock of the Wedgwood & Bentley partnership was sold at Christie's (then Christie & Ansell), London, much of it realized lower prices than those charged the previous year in Wedgwood's London showrooms. During the early part of the 19th century, and again for nearly 40 years of the present century, Wedgwood's jasper and basalt were sold for much lower prices than those realized in the previous 30 years. Neo-classical ornament does not appeal equally to all generations.

Fairyland Lustre was disregarded or condemned as vulgarly over-decorated for nearly 30 years before its revival in the 1960s. The early printed or painted creamwares, simple, elegant, and sometimes thought to be a little austere, are now generally undervalued. The heavily ornamented and decorated wares of the later Victorian period are still neglected, although majolica pieces are beginning to attract considerable interest. As some buyers of Impressionist and Post-Impressionist paintings discovered a few years ago, collectors who buy primarily for investment may be severely disappointed,

wedgwood
WEDGWOOD

Impressed: the letters being stamped individually and sometimes in a curve. The first marks, irregularly used c. 1759-69. Much of the Wedgwood of this period was unmarked.

WEDGWOOD

Impressed, in varying sizes, on useful wares from 1769-80, and on all wares from 1780 onwards unless otherwise stated below.

Impressed. The earliest form of the Wedgwood & Bentley mark. Ornamental wares only, c. 1769.

Impressed or raised, sometimes lacking the word ETRURIA, this mark appears on the inside corner of plinths of early basalt vases, and sometimes on the pedestals of busts and large figures, 1769-80.

Circular stamp, with an inner and outer line, always placed round the screw of basalt granite and Etruscan vases, 1769-80. Never on jasper vases, but sometimes found on white jasper plinths of granite vases.

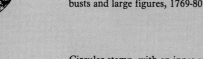

Extremely rare script mark, 1769-80, ornamental wares only.

Wedgwood
& Bentley
356

Impressed on very small cameos and intaglios, 1769-80, with the Catalogue number.

W. & B.

Impressed. Used on very small cameos and intaglios with the Catalogue number. Sometimes the Catalogue number only was used.

Rare oval impressed mark found only on chocolate and white seal intaglios, usually portraits made of two layers of jasper with polished edges.

WEDGWOOD
& BENTLEY
WEDGWOOD &
BENTLEY
ETRURIA

Impressed mark on plaques, tablets, medallions and other ornamental wares. The addition of ETRURIA is uncommon.

Wedgwood.

Impressed mark, varying in size, used for all types of ware from 1780 until c. 1795. Known as the 'upper and lower case' mark (or simply 'lower case').

WEDGWOOD & SONS

Impressed mark, c. 1790. Very rare

JOSIAH WEDGWOOD
Feb. 2nd 1805

Rare mark found on some lustre wares, and basalts and jasper pieces, usually tripods.

WEDGWOOD

Printed on bone china c. 1812-22, in red, blue or gold.

WEDGWOOD'S
STONE CHINA

Printed on stone china, 1820-61.

WEDGWOOD
ETRURIA

Impressed mark in various sizes, c. 1840-45.

PEARL
P

Impressed 'PEARL' on pearl body c. 1840-68; initial 'P' only thereafter.

JBS

Impressed three-letter marks were used to date earthenwares from 1860-1906. The first letter indicated the month, the second the potter, and the third the year. As may be seen from the table below, the third letter may indicate two possible dates for the years 1860-64 and 1886-90. After 1891 the word ENGLAND was added. The words MADE IN ENGLAND appear from c. 1898 but were not in general use until about 1908. The example shown, JBS, indicates a date of January 1864 or 1890.

Code (first) letters for months:

January	J		July	V		(1860-63)
February	F			L		(1864-1907)
March	M	(1860-63)	August	W		
	R	(1864-1907)	September	S		
April	A		Octover	O		
May	Y	(1860-63)	November	N		
	M	(1864-1907)	December	D		
June	T					

Code (third) letters for years are:

A	1872	1898	N		1885	
B	1873	1899	O	1860	1886	
C	1874	1900	P	1861	1887	
D	1875	1901	Q	1862	1888	
E	1876	1902	R	1863	1889	
F	1877	1903	S	1864	1890	
G	1878	1904	T	1865	1891	
H	1879	1905	U	1866	1892	
I	1880	1906	V	1867	1893	
J	1881		W	1868	1894	
K	1882		X	1869	1895	
L	1883		Y	1870	1896	
M	1884		Z	1871	1897	

From 1907 the figure 3 was substituted for the first (month) letter. From 1924 the figure 4 was used. The last letter continued to indicate the year as shown below:

J(3)	1907	V	1919
K	1908	W	1920
L	1909	X	1921
M	1910	Y	1922
N	1911	Z	1923
O	1912	A (4)	1924
P	1913	B	1925
Q	1914	C	1926
R	1915	D	1927
S	1916	E	1928
T	1917	F	1929
U	1918		

From 1930 the actual date was impressed, at first as the last two figures of a mark including the month numbered in sequence and a potter's mark (e.g. 3B35 = March 1935) and later simply as two figures (e.g. 57 = 1957).

Workmen's errors occur in the numbers and letters of marks 18 and 19, and the letters are not always legible.

 Signature of Emile Lessore c. 1858-76.

ENGLAND

Impressed or printed from 1891 to conform with McKinley Tariff Act. 'Made in England' added from c. 1898, but not invariably used until c. 1908

WEDGWOOD

Printed on bone china (and occasionally, and probably in error, on Queen's ware) from 1878. 'England' added below from 1891. Some bone china bears the standard Wedgwood impressed mark.

WEDGWOOD
ETRURIA ENGLAND

Rarely found impressed on Queen's ware c. 1891-1900.

MADE IN ENGLAND

Impressed or printed with standard WEDGWOOD mark from c. 1898, but not in general use until c. 1908.

WEDGWOOD

Printed on bone china from c. 1900 with ENGLAND or MADE IN ENGLAND added below.

WEDGWOOD
BONE CHINA
MADE IN ENGLAND

Printed on bone china from c. 1902 (BONE CHINA added).

 a. Painted monogram of Alfred Powell

 b. Painted monogram of Louise Powell

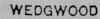
WEDGWOOD

Sans serif type impressed from 1929. The old type continued to be used for a short time after this date, but no sans serif marks were used before 1929.

WEDGWOOD
BONE CHINA
MADE IN ENGLAND

Rejafix machine-printed mark used on bone china from c. 1950-62.

WEDGWOOD
Bone China
MADE IN ENGLAND

Improved bone china mark introduced in 1962.

of ETRURIA
WEDGWOOD
MADE IN ENGLAND
BARLASTON

Queen's ware printed mark from c. 1940.

BARLASTON

Address of the firm added to standard marks from 1940.

N W
or
NORMAN WILSON

Impressed or painted on Norman Wilson Unique Ware, added to standard mark for the period.

ENGRAVED BY
WEDGWOOD
STUDIO

Printed on engraved patterns from 1952.

WEDGWOOD
ETRURIA
BARLASTON

Extremely rare mark impressed on basalt vases, replicas of those laid in the foundations of the factory at Barlaston in September 1938.

buying at the peak of prices dictated by fashion, and having to sell when the fashion has changed.

The price history of the Wedgwood jasper replicas of the Portland vase is not typical of the course of Wedgwood prices, but it is instructive of the fluctuations that may occur. The following examples are all for first edition vases:

1790 (date of issue)	£35	1956	£480
1849	£20	1963	£1,417
1859	£133	1964	£3,045
1889	£131	1971	£20,000
1902	£399	1974	£18,000 (slightly imperfect)
1923	£110 (Prince Regent's copy)	1975	£18,000

Other comparisons are likely to be misleading because old auction records seldom provided essential details of condition or estimated date of manufacture. Pairs of Wedgwood & Bentley Wine & Water ewers (Plate 147) sold at auction in 1781 for less than £2, for £27 in 1866, and for £5,460 in 1975. At the other end of the scale, 18th century hand-painted Queen's ware plates are still to be found for less than $22.

Pieces with a respectable provenance, or which are known to have come from distinguished collections, generally fetch higher prices than those which are unaccompanied by supporting documentary evidence, and armorial or masonic wares are always of special interest. In all comparisons of prices it is necessary to take into account the devaluation of currencies, particularly that of Britain during the past 20 years. In real terms, many of the finest works of art and craftsmanship now change hands for less than their prices in the 19th century.

Damage affects prices, particularly in the case of fairly common examples. Chipped or cracked pieces are likely to appeal more to the scholarly collector than to those who collect for aesthetic pleasure or investment. Firecracks (often erroneously described as 'age cracks') must be distinguished from cracks due to damage.

Firecracks, which are always wider at one end, are usually caused by faulty design, resulting in cracking or distortion in firing. They are not, by themselves, sufficient reason for rejecting a specimen that is otherwise desirable.

The techniques of the skilled restorer have now reached such a high standard that repairs may be invisible without the aid of a powerful magnifier or X-ray equipment. Responsible dealers will always draw attention to repairs and accept the return of pieces later found to have been repaired. Fine restoration work is always costly and it is generally unwise for the collector to buy specimens requiring extensive restoration unless they are of great rarity.

The collector relies upon three main sources: private sellers, dealers and auction rooms. Buying privately, the collector must trust his own knowledge or put his confidence in the owner. Even specialist dealers make errors, and general dealers often do not have the detailed knowledge that would enable them to describe all their goods accurately.

The large auction houses, who employ specialists in each department (and often take advice from consultants), generally provide both accurate descriptions and sensible estimates of price.

In the past 25 years, spectacular and well-publicized rises in the prices paid for antiques and works of art have brought into the market a vast number of so-called collectors, who have little appreciation of art or craftsmanship, and whose sole motive is quick cash profit. To supply them, an artificial market has been created, founded upon extensive advertising and often totally misleading claims to quality, rarity and investment potential. A flourishing sector of this market is that of the illusory limited edition: either an edition, genuinely limited in quantity, but of goods so over-priced and of such inferior quality that they would be unsaleable at the price advertised by any other means; or an edition produced in such quantity that the description 'limited' is delusive. Unless such goods have some intrinsic value (as, for instance, platinum or gold), they are valuable only to the extent to which they possess those features that make objects desirable to a collector. These features are: beauty, quality of art or craftsmanship, rarity, and historical significance. A depressingly large proportion of the objects offered in so-called limited editions possess none of these and are therefore of no interest to the collector. They do, however, sometimes appeal to the uninformed investor. For the collector who has no confidence in his knowledge or taste, a simple form of insurance is to buy only those objects which carry an internationally accepted hallmark of quality. For more than 200 years the name of Wedgwood has been synonymous with quality of craftsmanship, and the Wedgwood trademark has come to be recognized as a guarantee of integrity.

Luck, or chance, plays a part in every collector's life, but there are more collectors impoverished by failure to take advantage of opportunities than enriched by luck. One of the most celebrated of American collectors of Wedgwood made many of his own opportunities. The late Harry M. Buten used to advertise in the *Times* of London that he would be 'travelling clockwise' round Britain between certain dates, and invite people who wished to sell Wedgwood wares to make contact with him at his London hotel. He founded the Buten Museum of Wedgwood in Philadelphia, and this collection, which is open to the public, now contains some 10,000 exhibits, the most comprehensive range of Wedgwood wares to be seen anywhere in the world. Harry Buten began his collection with the modest purchase of a small lustre jug in 1931.

A fine collection is the product of study, perseverance, experience and discrimination. Collecting may be an intellectual exercise or an aesthetic experience, or at its best a happy combination of both, but the great collections have been founded upon a union of knowledge and understanding. The appreciation of quality, in design and craftsmanship, is the indispensable equipment of the genuine collector. The varied and endlessly fascinating wares produced by Wedgwood during more than 200 years of demonstrating the art of the potter provide an unrivaled field for the exercise of discriminating taste.

5 The Care of Wedgwood

It is a popular misapprehension that objects of pottery and porcelain are particularly fragile and delicate. Owners who will happily ruin an 18th century oil painting by 'giving it a good wash,' or a watercolor by exposing it to direct sunlight, or an antique bronze by 'cleaning' it with metal polish, will lock away their porcelain behind glass, retrieving it with trembling hands once a year for washing. It is true that earthenware struck against a harder object is easily chipped, and dropped on a hard floor it stays dropped, but porcelain is very strong, and neither pottery nor porcelain demand more than ordinary care and sensible handling. The exceptional strength of bone china was publicly demonstrated in 1958 when a red double-decker London Transport bus was successfully mounted on four Wedgwood teacups without damage to the cups, or the bus.

Cleaning

All modern Wedgwood decoration undergoes stringent tests in the laboratories at Barlaston, and it is safe to wash it with most household detergents. It is also generally considered safe in domestic dishwashing machines, but this is not recommended here because the design of some machines, or the careless use of them, may result in abrasion of gold or overglaze enamel decoration, or in scratching of the glaze. The finest tableware is costly to buy, but it is not expensive in comparison with other household furnishings. It is manufactured to last for a lifetime, requiring no expenditure on maintenance. In these terms it is one of the most attractive investments available.

The care of antique Wedgwood is simple if a few elementary rules are followed. The first, and most important, is to examine the article carefully to identify the type of ceramic body and look for signs of damage. Methods of cleaning vary according to the composition of the ware and its condition. Each of the different bodies described in Chapter Three requires appropriate methods of cleaning.

Earthenware

All *undamaged* Queen's ware, Pearl ware and majolica may be washed in warm soapy water or a very weak solution of detergent, though care must be taken in the use of detergents since too strong a solution may damage glazes or lustre decoration. Objects should not be left to soak, and very hot water should be avoided. Since earthenware is porous, damaged pieces should not be immersed in water. They may be wiped with a damp cloth, squeezed out in soapy water, and then rubbed lightly with a clean soft cloth dampened with methylated spirit. Allow the spirit to dry and polish with a dry cloth, preferably silk, which will not deposit fluff on the surface.

Many stains, including those in crazing, will yield to treatment with magnesium silicate (known also as soap rock, soap stone and steatite). Soak the article in distilled water, allowing it to absorb as much as possible, and then coat the stained part with a thick paste of magnesium silicate and distilled water. After about 24 hours the paste will begin to crack and should be removed. For more stubborn stains a cotton swab dampened with a solvent (e.g. acetone, methylated spirit, white spirit, or surgical spirit) may prove effective, but it must be remembered that these solvents are highly inflammable and must be used in the open air or a well-ventilated room. The fumes of acetone, in particular, are dangerous if inhaled.

Stoneware

Black basalt should *never* be washed. Its beauty depends largely on the patina or 'bloom' resulting from years of polishing with a soft cloth, and this is instantly destroyed by water. The polish of a piece which has become dull or dirty from long neglect can be restored by rubbing with the palm of the hand (remembering to remove any rings on the fingers because basalt is a touchstone for gold), or a soft cloth, preferably silk. If the piece has been washed it will appear gray and lifeless. In this case the polish may be more quickly restored by the use of refined oil or a microcrystalline wax polish, applied very sparingly on a cloth or a soft brush. Great care must be taken to avoid the greasy or sticky sheen resulting from too generous an application or oil or wax, and ordinary wax polishes, which may contain unsuitable ingredients, are not recommended.

Plain cane ware with engine-turned decoration or applied ornament may be scrubbed with a soft brush in warm soapy water. Enameled or gilded cane should not be washed, but it may be dusted with a very soft brush (artists' watercolor brushes are particularly suitable) or a clean soft cloth.

Jasper should be washed in warm soapy water, and if very dirty may be scrubbed with a bristle brush (e.g., soft nail brush or toothbrush). It must be rinsed well, preferably in distilled water.

Rosso antico with white relief ornament may be washed like jasper, but if the reliefs are of black basalt the piece should be dusted but never washed (see Black Basalt above).

Drab ware of either the stoneware or earthenware variety may be washed in warm soapy water, and a soft brush may be used for ornamented pieces.

Porcelain

All porcelain may be washed safely in warm soapy water, and many stains will yield to treatment with damp salt or bicarbonate of soda left for two hours and then rinsed thoroughly. More stubborn stains may be treated with a weak solution of hydrogen peroxide. First soak the article in distilled water for about two hours. Then apply a pad soaked in a solution of hydrogen peroxide (one part to three parts water if 100 vols. hydrogen peroxide is used) with a drop of ammonia added. Hydrogen peroxide, and other bleaching agents, may damage the glaze, so the solution must be weak and the pad must not be left in place for more than two hours at a time. It is wise to remove the pad at 30-minute intervals to examine the glaze under a glass for any signs of roughening. The process may be repeated until the stain disappears. Household bleach should never be used for this purpose because it may produce crazing, and care must be exercised not to allow bleach of any kind to come into contact with gold or lustre decoration.

309

Carrara (Parian) may be cleaned with a weak ammonia solution. Rubber gloves should be worn to avoid irritation to the skin, and work should always be carried out in the open air or a well-ventilated room.

Restoration

The restoration of valuable antique pottery and porcelain is a job for an expert and should not be attempted by enthusiastic amateurs. The development of epoxy resin adhesives has made possible the permanent repair of broken pieces, but it is well to remember that such repairs, imperfectly carried out, may be more permanent than satisfying. Epoxy resin adhesives should never be used on porous bodies because they are liable to create irremediable discoloration under the glaze. It is seldom wise for collectors to try to restore old Wedgwood ware without professional advice and help. With patience and some manual dexterity, a collector may learn the craft of pottery restoration, and there are many practical courses of study available. Time spent in such study under professional tutelage will save many hours of frustration and regret for slightly damaged articles that have been irretrievably ruined.

Records and Display

Every acquisition to a collection should be catalogued in a ledger or on index cards. The details recorded should always include a full description of the type of ware, color, decoration, size, marks, date, price and provenance. It is wise to leave plenty of room for further details, such as notes of further research (which may include the identification of the artist or designer) and reference to similar pieces illustrated or described in standard books on the subject or in sale catalogues, or to examples in museums. A photograph, or negative reference number, is helpful for identification and for insurance purposes.

The display of a collection is essentially a matter of personal taste, but some brief observations may be helpful to collectors of limited experience. There are, unhappily, collections which are crammed into locked, glass-fronted cabinets, often no more than three feet in height. Those pieces near the front may be viewed with difficulty from a distance, or at close quarters by adopting an attitude more suitable for prayer: the remainder cannot be seen at all. The purpose served by such a collection, or the pleasure derived by its owner, are not easy to imagine. There is a great divide between a collection and an accumulation; and between display and storage. In all collections one fine and interesting piece which can be shown to its best advantage is preferable to 40 pieces of inferior quality for which there is inadequate room. Beauty of form is the first virtue of much Wedgwood ware, and it must be given sufficient space. Much of the pleasure of collecting lies in sharing a collection with other enthusiasts. It must, therefore, be visible and accessible to people who can be trusted to handle it with sensitivity, and safe from the depredations of those who cannot. Attractive and suitable display is an important, but often neglected, facet of collecting, which adds much to the appearance of a collection and thus to the lasting pleasure of its owner.